Angry Young Women

six writers of the sixties

ANNE WELLMAN

Table of Contents

Introduction...1

A Taste of Honey *Shelagh Delaney*.......................................5

The L-Shaped Room *Lynne Reid Banks*............................61

The Pumpkin Eater *Penelope Mortimer*...........................95

Up the Junction and Poor Cow *Nell Dunn*....................125

The Millstone *Margaret Drabble*.......................................177

Georgy Girl *Margaret Forster*...207

Afterword...245

Bibliography 255

Introduction

A Taste of Honey, The L-Shaped Room, The Pumpkin Eater, Up the Junction, Poor Cow, The Millstone, and *Georgy Girl*: works that are seen as defining radical female literature in 1960s Britain. All of the authors were young. Their writing spread beyond their native shores to be just as eagerly consumed in America, Canada, Australasia and indeed around the world. Every one of these iconic works was made into a film, most of them equally iconic, if not more so.

Shelagh Delaney. Lynne Reid Banks. Penelope Mortimer. Nell Dunn. Margaret Drabble. Margaret Forster. Each of these writers, at one time or another, was labelled an 'Angry Young Woman'. The tag arose in reference to the so-called 'Angry Young Men' of the 1950s, a loose grouping of young male writers characterised by a sense of disillusionment with traditional British society, particularly the class system: most were from working-class backgrounds, the first group of writers not to come from the middle or upper classes or to have been to university. In an attempt to achieve political change these young men created characters who rebelled against class barriers and everything else they hated about staid, hidebound 1950s Britain. Earning the group its nickname was John Osborne's play *Look Back in Anger,* a kitchen sink drama about the unhappy existence of an intelligent, angry young working-class man and his upper-class wife in a squalid flat. Shelagh Delaney, author of the play *A Taste of Honey,* was the first of the female writers to whom the phrase was applied, on that occasion by a *Daily Mail* theatre critic reviewing the play's opening performance in 1958. 'She knows what she is angry about,' the programme for the production likewise declared. But what was it?

Shelagh's writing almost at the start of the decade, and that of the other young women as the 1960s played out, was about the realities of being female during the second half of the twentieth century. A new excitement was in the air: the economy was thriving, the class system was beginning to splinter and there was a growing realisation that women had a right to the same things as men, including in matters of sex. But real life was a different affair, and the consequences of sex the same as they ever had been. Women knew very little about their own bodies and contraception was a word too explicit and rude even to be mentioned. The pill was available on the NHS from 1961, but for many years doctors and clinics would prescribe it only to married women. Abortion remained illegal until 1967 but nevertheless took place, frequently and dangerously. The actuality was therefore that despite the new era, young women were far from free, still in thrall to biology and liable to become pregnant. Pregnancy, abortion, childbirth, and motherhood: still the realities of life, and the subjects these 'Angry Young Women' chose to write about – plus the added new possibility of raising a child alone.

The central parts in the movie versions were played by the decade's rising young stars – Rita Tushingham, Carol White, Lynn Redgrave – as well as established favourites such as Leslie Caron and Anne Bancroft. All the directors were men, who for the most part distorted the original intention of the play or novel and produced films different in tone and detail but in some cases almost more celebrated.

This is the story of these pivotal works: how they came to be written by those women at that time, what was meant, how they were received and translated into film – and how some of these writers ultimately viewed their work across the span of years.

But were they really 'Angry Young Women'?

A Taste of Honey

Shelagh Delaney

PETER: *Look at Helen, isn't she a game old bird? Worn out on the beat but she's still got a few good strokes left.*

HELEN: *Get out of here, you drunken sot.*

A Taste of Honey, Shelagh Delaney, 1958

§

The teenaged writer of the above, Shelagh Delaney, was born in Salford, near Manchester, to mother Elsie and a father who worked on the buses. It was late 1938 and Salford was still a very deprived city, the lives of many of its citizens blighted by poor housing, poor food and poor air from industrial pollution. The week of Shelagh's birth the city was taking part in National Rat Week: the *Salford City Reporter* revealed that in the previous two years rat-catchers in the city had caught 2,261 live rats and destroyed thousands more.

The Second World War was also rapidly approaching. Fourteen nurses were to die in the blitz in the hospital where Shelagh was born, and her childhood was defined by wartime privations and the sights and sounds of a country in conflict: sirens and searchlights, gas masks and air raid shelters. Her determined mother Elsie refused to allow her daughter to be evacuated. Her half-Irish father Joe, a great reader and storyteller, joined the Army but after being badly wounded was invalided out and back at home by 1943, vividly recounting his experiences in North Africa to an enthralled young Shelagh.

After the war the family – now with the addition of Shelagh's younger brother Joe – were moved away from the city's dockland area to a pleasant council house in the suburbs, allocated to them because of Joe's invalid status and because of his public sector job on the buses. It was a wrench for them all, leaving the lively, companionable streets they were used to for a quiet and lonely new neighbourhood. Shelagh had to attend a new school and for the first time felt herself a stranger, an outsider. Beneath her wild black hair she had grown tall and thin, at age nine already five feet five inches at a time when the average adult woman was only just over five feet. Her height made her self-conscious and inclined to stoop. At the new school the teachers considered the awkward, dislocated young girl to be disposed to 'sullenness'.

When she was ten Shelagh contracted osteomyelitis, a painful and life-threatening infection which atatcked the bones of her leg. Part of the cure was rest, and she was sent to a children's convalescent home in Lytham St Annes, two hours away by train from Salford. Here she was given a room of her own at the top of the house with a view of the sea through an iron-barred window. The home was run by an order of strict Catholic nuns who according to Shelagh stinted on the meals supplied to the inmates and would hoard food: she claimed to have investigated the cellars and found them filled with bins of bread and sacks of vegetables.

Shelagh later wrote a semi-autobiographical story about this period of her life. The narrator, a young girl, is frightened to be so many miles away from her family but is perceptive enough to examine her own state of mind: '...when I try to find a cause of being frightened I can't and begin to think it is not fear I feel at all but something else.' She notices that while the home is supposed to make children healthier, many have been there for years and don't look any the better for it, in which case it is hopeless and she herself is doomed. The food is poor, sometimes just a cup of cocoa and a slice of bread and jam for a meal instead of the kind of hearty fare the girl is used to from her mother: potato pie, red cabbage and gravy, apple crumble and custard. She's the tallest, thinnest girl in the place, and is plied with iron pills and cod-liver oil to build her up. For all the inmates there are long rests and bracing walks along the shore; the seaside in winter is 'lonely and quiet in a way I have never come across before'. The library is out of bounds and there is no music or radio. On asking for a book to enliven the boredom and being given the Bible, the girl in the story retorts that she has already read it. She wants to read and write rather than occupy herself with sewing, and at one point goes on strike and downs tools; questioned by the nuns the girl caustically replies that she is reflecting on the Sufferings of St John of the Cross. She is unusually mature for her years and understands, for example, that one child's reported abuse by her father was not just cruelty but in fact incest, and that this should not be spelt out for the other children.

Although only semi-autobiographical, the narrator's experiences can be assumed to be based on Shelagh's difficult and lonely sojourn at the convalescent home. Along with the other children there Shelagh also received the 'sun-ray' treatment in common use at the time, half-dressed sessions under an ultraviolet lamp administered in the belief that the rays were curative and would get unwell children back on their feet. Decades later it would of course transpire that nothing could have been more harmful, with scores of such children being diagnosed with dangerous skin cancer when mature adults.

Shelagh was eventually well enough to go home, and back to school. Her education at primary level had already been disrupted by the frequent moves made by her family during the war, and it was no doubt hard to recover lost time. She failed her 11-plus – the exam determining entrance either to the more academic grammar schools or the alternative secondary moderns – apparently more than once. She later claimed that her father rang up the town hall and was informed that she had actually gained the marks to pass, but could not be admitted to a grammar as there were insufficient places. She was sent therefore to a local secondary modern school, but at the age of fifteen was transferred to Pendleton High School for Girls when the local Education Committee asked secondary school heads to submit promising children for transfer. Shelagh herself modestly ascribed the move to being 'a bit more cheeky than the rest, a bit more conspicuous', although in fact of course her intelligence had been recognised, particularly her aptitude for English. For Shelagh's maths teacher, while conceding that her pupil was hopeless at arithmetic, '...there was something so special about her that Salford Education Committee made a very special exception'.

Arriving at the imposing grammar school, Shelagh was initially nervous about knowing a great deal less than the other pupils but later claimed to discover she knew a 'damn sight more'. She felt sorry for the boys and girls she had left behind at the secondary, half of whom she thought just as capable as herself but who were destined to leave school at fifteen. Educational segregation at age eleven was wrong, she believed. She was to obtain five good GCE passes at Pendleton.

Teachers there remembered her as someone who stood out from the rest. 'You could always talk to Shelagh as a grown-up,' recalled the history mistress after her former pupil had found fame. 'She was very mature even when she came to us...quick to debunk the other girls' awful silliness about boyfriends and makeup'. Contemporaries at Pendleton recalled her as a netball star, a form captain and natural leader who had a crew of friends and, in contravention of school rules, would play ragtime on the school's grand piano. She was a frequent rule-breaker, in fact, sometimes skipping classes to wander around Salford, and a general free spirit and champion of the underdog: at one point she was involved in getting a group of bullies expelled. By this time Shelagh was confident in who she was, though still self-conscious about her height. For Salford her looks were unconventional: a thick, glossy black mane of hair topping sallow skin.

As for the future, she was sure of at least one thing. Having seen her mother go out to work in a factory and then come home at the end of the day to tend to her invalid husband and make the tea before she even sat down, by her mid-teens Shelagh was declaring to her friends that she would never marry. A good listener and increasingly interested in other people's lives, she was also a budding writer, contributing to the school magazine and remembered by one friend as bringing a notepad and pencil to take notes when on a visit to the friend's family. However, she was no academic. There were no thoughts of further education once school had been abandoned after just two terms in the sixth form. She was not an intellectual, Shelagh was to maintain, describing herself as 'more intelligent than intellectual' and lacking in the discipline necessary to a scholar. A succession of mundane jobs ensued: a brief period in a smart dress shop – which she hated – office girl in a milk depot, usherette at Manchester Opera House (sacked for fraternising with the actors, said Shelagh), and then a post in the research lab at engineering company Metropolitan-Vickers Electrical.

But all the while Shelagh intended to write, which she had wanted to since at least sixteen:

I knew I could, by comparing my essays with the ones the other girls wrote at school.

She labelled her state of mind at seventeen as a 'terrible mess', not knowing what to do with her life. But the series of low-level jobs had at least opened up some ideas about the future, in particular her stint at the opera house where she was able to watch the plays as long as she remembered to leave before the interval to serve the ice-creams. Shelagh's interest in the theatre had already been awakened at the secondary modern school, where at the age of twelve she had been very impressed by an amateur performance of *Othello* (and would later include lines from Shakespeare in *A Taste of Honey*). The headmistress at the school there had encouraged her in her writing, accepting what she produced without insisting on formal English. At Pendleton her interest had continued to grow. Her class was taken to see Laurence Olivier in *Antony and Cleopatra* and also performances of Shakespeare and Chekhov put on by the pupils at Salford Grammar, where she met the later artist Harold Riley, then a schoolboy actor playing the title role in *Henry IV Part I*. Harold liked Shelagh's wit and intelligence and strong character, and over the many years of their friendship – or perhaps more than friendship, according to the adult Harold – the two would often go to the cinema and theatre together or hang out at a local café listening to the jukebox.

He was also impressed by Shelagh's knowledge of local theatre and her attempts at writing. She would show him some of her efforts, which could be frank. She lived in a tough district and saw what went on around her, Harold recalled:

She liked to shock. She had strong ideas about what she wanted to see in the theatre. She used to object to plays where factory workers come cap in hand and call the boss 'Sir'. Usually North Country people are shown as gormless, but [Shelagh] believed they were very alive and cynical.

The theatre was exerting an ever stronger attraction. By now Shelagh had seen and read quite a number of modern plays and had even done a little acting as a member of the amateur Salford Players. It was here that she met David Scase, artistic director of the Manchester Library Theatre Company, and asked him for advice on how to become a producer. He was unable to help, but suggested she come along to watch rehearsals and get a feel of the theatre. This Shelagh did, though without making any mention of her writing ambitions, so that the company were very surprised when she later emerged as a famous playwright.

§

In early 1958, at the astonishing age of only nineteen, Shelagh sent the script of *A Taste of Honey* to the radical, left-leaning director Joan Littlewood at Theatre Workshop in London. She had been advised to do so by David Scase, who knew Joan from a period she spent working in Salford theatre when a young woman. Joan's name had lately been in the public eye. The national press had reported her appearance in court for a production which contravened current censorship; her company was ordered to pay only a small fine, a victory of sorts. The canny Shelagh no doubt understood very well that the more conventional theatres in Salford and Manchester were unlikely to accept the kind of play she had written, and that it might well run into similar censorship trouble and need defending by someone exactly like Joan.

She wrote an accompanying letter, changing the spelling of her name from its original 'Sheila' in the mistaken belief that the new version was the Irish spelling (probably to reflect her Irish roots, which she was proud of). The letter was forthright, confident, and not altogether truthful:

Along with this letter comes a play, the first I have written. I wondered if you would read it through and send it back to me because no matter what sort of theatrical atrocity it might be, it isn't valueless so far as I'm concerned. A fortnight ago I didn't know the theatre existed, but a young man, anxious to improve my mind, took me to the Opera House in Manchester and I came away after the performance having suddenly realised that at last, after nineteen years of life, I had discovered something that meant more to me than myself. I sat down and thought...I set to and produced this little epic – don't ask me why – I'm quite unqualified for anything like this...I want to write for the theatre, but I know so very little about it. I know nothing, have nothing – except a willingness to learn – and intelligence.

Shelagh had in fact been trying her hand at writing for quite some time and of course knew far more about the theatre than she made out. The letter to Joan Littlewood can be seen for what it is: the shrewd attempt of a young person to attract attention by presenting herself as untutored and naïve and – if her play impressed – therefore all the more of a genius.

It worked, although the play itself was astonishing and did not require much selling (and Joan was not immune to the lure of only five characters and a minimum of sets). She immediately accepted it for production – reportedly only the fourth to be taken on from the thousands sent to the company over the previous five years – and even took a two-year option on any further efforts. Shelagh just as promptly accepted Joan's invitation to attend rehearsals in London and handed in her notice at work. She arrived, unusually tall and wearing a man's white mac, and made a strong impression asking for a cup of tea in her deep, Northern voice. She found lodging partly with Mancunian actress and former music hall performer Avis Bunnage, who was to star in the play, and partly with Joan herself.

The play's title came from the Bible story about Saul's son Jonathan taking a single taste of honey when his father had ordered fasting and then being condemned to death for his transgression: the play's central character, teenaged Jo, must similarly pay a price for her brief dalliance with a boy in search of her own taste of honey. The themes of the play, and the language, were startling for the time. In the play as it is now published, seventeen-year-old Jo lives with her mother Helen, a crude and selfish woman who survives as a semi-prostitute. Jo is creative and likes to draw, but has given up any hope of becoming an artist. Mother and daughter have a complex, sniping relationship and have just moved into a shabby bedsit which Jo attempts to beautify with little touches, all the while carping at her mother for their drifting existence and Helen's predilection for sex and singing in pubs – Jo wants to get away and live her own life, with a job and a place to herself. Enter cocksure car salesman Peter, Helen's lover from whom she has run away but who now proposes marriage, much to Jo's scorn. After he leaves, Jo and Helen get ready for bed, and the scene ends with a confession from Jo that she is scared of the dark, not of the darkness outside but the 'darkness inside houses'.

The next scene finds Jo out on the street with her black boyfriend, a naval rating called Jimmie. They kiss and talk nonsense and Jimmie proposes marriage to his 'Honey'. Back inside the bedsit Helen reveals to Jo that her first husband divorced her because she was pregnant with Jo, another man's child. She has accepted Peter's proposal, who now arrives, and the two go off together following a hostile but also semi-flirtatious exchange between Peter and Jo, who is upset by the news of the marriage. Jimmie then turns up again and Jo lets him stay, knowing that nothing good will come of it.

Helen is then shown dressing for the wedding while Jo reveals that she too has had a proposal of marriage. An angry Helen asks why she doesn't learn from her mother's mistakes and discloses that Jo's father, now dead, was 'a bit stupid'. Jo, concerned that madness is hereditary, asks if she herself is mad ('Not more so than anybody else,' says Helen). She wishes her mother good luck.

In the following scene it is several months later, still in the bedsit, where a clearly pregnant Jo is living alone after Helen's departure. She is with her gay friend Geof, who has been thrown out of his own lodgings – with the implication that it is because of his sexuality – and is looking for a place to live. Jo allows him to move in and begins to depend on his cooking, cleaning and caring as her pregnancy advances. She is ambivalent about her approaching motherhood. Geof wants to try a physical relationship but is rejected, and then Helen, accompanied by a drunk and quarrelsome Peter, reappears on the scene. Helen promises to send money every week, then offers Jo a home with her and Peter but is turned down. An enraged Peter refuses any such idea and forces Helen to leave with him.

In the final scene Jo is close to giving birth. She has been worrying about her 'daft' father again and is conflicted as regards the coming child:

I'll bash its brains out. I'll kill it. I don't want his baby, Geof.
I don't want to be a mother. I don't want to be a woman.

A Taste of Honey, Shelagh Delaney, 1958

Helen now returns for good, having been abandoned by Peter for another woman; she drives 'bloody little pansy' Geof away from the flat. Jo goes into labour and reveals to a dismayed Helen that the baby will be black. Her mother leaves to find a drink – promising she'll be back – and the play ends with Jo left on her own, singing a nursery rhyme taught her by Geof.

It sounds bleak, and it is, but it is mainly very funny. '[W]hat's wrong with this place?' asks Helen of Jo about their bare new bedsit. 'Everything in it's falling apart, it's true, and we've no heating – but there's a lovely view of the gasworks, we share a bathroom with the community and this wallpaper's contemporary. What more do you want?' It was also highly original: couched in Salford dialect, set variously in a squalid bedsit and by the side of a canal, and, most radical of all, written from the point of view of women who have minds of their own and want a lot more out of life than just marriage and babies, even if these things do happen to them. Their desire is for love, adventure, creativity, escape from the mundane: a taste of honey. In fact originally Shelagh had created solely these two female characters, mother and daughter, with their complex relationship the central feature of the play, but then realised as she was writing that the play required other people for the duo to fully reveal themselves.

But most of all it was shocking for the late 1950s – a whorish mother, a teenage pregnancy, a black boyfriend, homosexuality: the script was scandalous, saying things out loud that were generally whispered. Director Joan Littlewood liked it and understood its potential, but had her reservations. While recognising the raw power of Shelagh's writing she could still see that the script was incoherent and badly structured, with little in the way of plot. She determined to use Shelagh's work as a basis for improvisation by her team of talented actors, as she often did with her productions, in order to arrive at a more finished product through the process of collaboration. Some of the actors themselves had different ideas. Avis Bunnage, playing Helen, had initially refused the role, disliking the play and commenting that Shelagh (whom she had not yet met) needed 'a swift kick up the arse'.

Joan also played up the work's existing vaudeville aspects, adding radical new devices such as having Helen talk directly to the audience and organising live jazz music to set the mood, link the scenes and play individual signature tunes for each character as they came and went – innovations borrowed from music hall, which had the effect of subverting an otherwise naturalistic play and acting as a challenge to legitimate theatre. Joan liked the way the music smoothed over abrupt scene changes by allowing characters to *dance* from one scene to the next, and also to sing and dance in the middle of the action. She had the jazz band sitting in one of the theatre's ornate boxes beside the stage and the actors would talk and joke with them; during these interactions the audience's eyes would turn away from the stage to look at the players, thereby destroying any illusion of 'reality' and transgressing yet another rule of theatre. However, this radical treatment somehow made the action *more* real, the actors recalled, revealing the 'truth of the thing' – realism achieved by non-realistic means and seen as Joan's answer to the rise of television, which did not allow for communication between actors and audience. She was all for a return to Elizabethan theatre with audiences screaming out or throwing oranges if they didn't like the action: a truly collective and egalitarian experience.

She had creative ways of getting the best out of her actors. To rehearse the opening scene of the play, when mother and daughter arrive at their grim new lodgings carrying suitcases, she told Avis and Frances Cuka as Jo to tramp round and round the stage with the suitcases full of weights until the two were at daggers drawn with each other and no longer speaking to Joan either – at which point Joan ordered them to start the play. Avis and Frances then gave the opening lines, with mother and daughter viciously snapping at each other, all the pent-up rage and frustration they had just accumulated. Joan also had Avis and Nigel Davenport as her boyfriend Peter genuinely drunk for the scenes in which they are meant to be inebriated, and would generally throw the odd spanner into the works so that the action would appear made up as it went along. Joan could be a pain, and make you suffer, Frances Cuka remembered – but she had 'immense stage craft'.

Nineteen-year-old Shelagh was apparently happy to submit to Joan's collaborative process. She was involved in the re-writing throughout – despite Joan claiming in her memoirs that Shelagh never noticed the differences between her draft and the adaptation – and in the future she would have nothing but good to say about her mentor Joan. In the opinion of actor Murray Melvin, who played Geof, Joan was an oddball and Shelagh was an oddball too – they liked each other and got on well.

Before hitting the stage for real the play had to be submitted to censors at the Lord Chamberlain's office, as were all plays at that period, and with its abrasive subject matter the script was likely to fall foul of decency standards then in force. However, times were just on the cusp of change. A recent top-level report on homosexual offences and prostitution in modern Britain, for example, had recommended that homosexual acts between consenting adults in private should no longer be a criminal offence, and in light of this new principle the censors would have needed to reconsider their views on the depiction of homosexuality. In the event the Lord Chamberlain's assistant thought the play 'revolting, quite apart from the homosexual bits' and the characters to be 'a sad collection of undesirables'. However, it was granted a licence, on the condition that certain phrases such as 'castrated little clown' (in relation to Geof) be removed, and later also that a phrase relating to Helen, 'Worn out but still a good few pumps left in her', be altered. Geof's overt homosexuality was additionally required to be toned down, although for at least some in the office the play dealt with 'the forbidden subject' of homosexuality in a way that nobody could object to.

A Taste of Honey made its debut on 27 May 1958 at the small Theatre Royal Stratford East, publicised beforehand as written by a nineteen-year-old 'factory worker from Salford, Lancashire' (not quite true – Shelagh was a photographic technician, not on an assembly line, but the description had greater street credibility). By this point the company was so broke it had no stage management, and the actors themselves had to see to the props, do the sound effects and electrics and ring down the curtain. When the old ditty *The big ship sails on the alley alley oh* – popularly thought to be about the Manchester Ship Canal – was sung offstage, it was Avis Bunnage and the wardrobe mistress doing the singing.

Joan was nervous: unmarried pregnancy, frank homosexuality and mixed-race relationships were completely new to the British stage. Murray Melvin playing the obviously homosexual Geof was worried about the reaction to such a depiction too. The theatre manager had an exit strategy. 'If there's any trouble,' he told Murray and Frances, 'just split either side of the stage and I'll bring the iron [safety curtain] in.'

There was no trouble. The amazing noise heard at the end of the play was a roar of approval. *A Taste of Honey* was a resounding success, unexpectedly keeping Theatre Workshop up and running when closure had been threatening. Audiences flocked, with Joan's introduction of jazz perhaps a particular draw for the younger generation – jazz at the time being thought of as radical and rebellious. Its first two weeks lengthened into a magnificent six-week run and Joan was approached to transfer the production to the West End. *A Taste of Honey* duly opened at the larger Wyndham's Theatre in Charing Cross, where it became even more of a hit and ran for nearly a year, moving from the Wyndham to the Criterion in Piccadilly Circus. Shelagh's first ever work won the Charles Henry Foyle New Play Award for 1958, appeared

20

as one of publisher Methuen's series of modern plays along with those of celebrated writers like Bertolt Brecht and Brendan Behan, and went on to enjoy a successful run on Broadway with Angela Lansbury as the mother and eventually Joan Plowright as Jo. Angela, later famed for her starring role in the American TV series *Murder, She Wrote*, enjoyed playing her 'truly female' part and admired Shelagh's talent for writing female dialogue. The New York version, though, at least in the opinion of theatrical producer Oscar Lewenstein, was nothing like as original or unsentimental as the English production, which would 'almost certainly not have worked on Broadway'.

The play on Broadway was accompanied by American jazz musician Bobby Scott's original melody *A Taste of Honey*, at that point an instrumental-only version which was part of a suite of incidental music he had composed specifically for the production. As in London this music was jazzy, except for the *A Taste of Honey* theme itself, slow and poignant on classical strings. Various cover versions of the song started to appear, with added lyrics, including the most famous one by the Beatles in 1963.

British reviews were mixed – many, of course, professing astonishment at Shelagh's themes. Her play was 'the story of a trollop's daughter who has a baby by a Negro sailor and sets up house with an effeminate artist', wrote a delightedly outraged *Daily Mirror*. Shelagh was merely trying to shock, it was said. Did the father of the baby have to be black? Did Jo's friend have to be homosexual? asked one critic. A representative from the BBC drama department, sent to check it out, enjoyed the play but was amazed that 'such apparently moronic people' could be so moving. For the *Spectator*, the play was 'the inside story of a savage culture observed by a genuine cannibal'. Jo was 'a pregnant slut,' said the *Manchester Guardian*.

Some felt that without Joan Littlewood's interventions the play would have been nothing: 'I feel that played perfectly straight it would have been much too thin to hold the stage at all,' weighed in the *New Statesman*. An extended music hall sketch with no genuine character content, sniffed the *Times*, although conceding Shelagh's talent at turning the 'language of the streets' into living stage dialogue. The *Tatler* was similarly condescending, praising Miss Delaney's 'remarkably good ear for the language of the Lancashire backstreets where the inarticulate pride themselves on the straight flinging of the limited number of words at their disposal' but disliking the music hall aspects and labelling the Jo character 'half-witted' and that of Geof 'pansified'. More than a few thought the work unconvincing and immature, showing an adolescent contempt for logic or form or practicability upon a stage. 'Humorous', 'entertaining', and 'lively' it might be, some reviewers allowed, but at the same time decrying the play's incoherence and shambolic nature and declaring that Shelagh's characters seemed to bumble around to no purpose. Its author knew as much about adult behaviour as she did about elephants, wrote one reviewer. Acknowledging the drama's poignancy, integrity, and 'strength in its crudity', the Arts Council on application granted the play a limited guarantee against loss, but had serious reservations:

This is a good Bad Play. It seems to have been dashed off in pencil in a school exercise-book by a youngster who knows practically nothing about the theatre and rather more about life than she can presently digest...Miss Delaney writes with the confidence of sheer ignorance.

Part of the criticism probably derived from Shelagh's gender. The media of the day were now familiar with rebellious, working-class writers of the 'Angry Young Men' tribe, but completely unprepared for those of the opposite sex. Shelagh was almost certainly taken less seriously because she was a female writing about females – and often slyly assumed to be writing from personal knowledge into the bargain. How else did a nineteen-year-old know so much about the seamy side of life? was the insinuation. 'The honey cake is obviously baked out of personal experience,' thundered a Scottish review, castigating the play as a 'sin'. The reality, of course, was that Shelagh grew up the product of her environment, surrounded by independent women who had to work for a living and some of whom prostituted themselves or gave birth to black babies. These were the facts of that life.

Others saw far more in her. Director Lindsay Anderson dubbed the play a work of complete, exhilarating originality, a real escape from the middlebrow, middle-class vacuum of the West End, while Shelagh herself he described as a courageous, sensitive and outspoken person writing real contemporary poetry. The writing was salty and uncompromising to gasping point at times, said the *Daily Herald*, the treatment 'as unsentimental and refreshing as a cold bath'. The distinguished playwright Emlyn Williams welcomed the individuality, imagination and humour of the play, which he preferred to sleek American-style productions, and predicted that Shelagh would become a major playwright. Her first play was touching and funny, he observed, with the scene between Jo and her sailor boyfriend charming and offbeat. Respected author Graham Greene described the play as 'having all the freshness of Mr Osborne's *Look Back in Anger* and greater maturity', while the renowned and influential theatre critic Kenneth Tynan saw Shelagh as a portent, bringing real people to the stage 'joking and flaring and scuffling and eventually out of the zest for life she gives them, surviving'. She dealt joyfully with what in other hands could have been a tragic situation, he pointed out.

As these influencers weighed in, the play began to seem something very out of the ordinary: a groundbreaker reflective of contemporary reality in Britain, particularly for working-class women, and depicting such characters wholly without condescension.

§

Shelagh, at age nineteen, found her life totally changed. The publicity machine pushed her as the girl genius from the working classes and to start with Shelagh appeared happy to play up to the myth, although seemingly less so as time went on. In press interviews after her play took off she would talk not about her deep reading and knowledge of modern theatre, but about a childhood spent at Saturday morning cowboy films (the 'penny crush'), and at the Hippodrome. The genesis of *A Taste of Honey* became part of the legend, with Shelagh deliberately projecting an image of an ordinary young woman, not intellectual, who happened to see a Terence Rattigan play and suddenly decided she could do a better job herself. (She had also been influenced by witnessing a badly attended and unappreciated production of Samuel Beckett's very experimental *Waiting for Godot*, which at the start of her career she did not usually include as part of the tale.) She began the play as a novel, she told the *Times* in 1959, but 'was too busy enjoying myself, going out dancing' to make it work. The play she had seen was the upper-middle-class Rattigan's *Variation on a Theme*, which featured homosexuality although only covertly. Rattigan's piece, said Shelagh, was about 'safe, cultured lives in charming surroundings'; to her it seemed merely an opportunity for its star Margaret Leighton to 'traipse about in Mr Norman Hartnell's creations...I felt she was wasting her time. I just went home and started work.' She took a fortnight off work to do so, her oft-repeated story went. When *A Taste of Honey* turned out to be a success she told a reporter that it was seeing the bricklayers and the cabbies going to her play that meant most to her.

The papers came up with the 'Angry Young Woman' label, seeing in Shelagh the first female to follow in the footsteps of the decade's 'Angry Young Men' and painting her as a beatnik who smoked cigars and liked a drink (all true). She gave numerous, often cynical-seeming interviews. 'It's rather a sordid theme,' said a plummy-voiced TV reporter about the play. 'Where did you get your information?' 'I just applied me imagination to me observation,' replied Shelagh drily. The girl from Salford – six foot tall and with her dark good looks, extremely striking – became a national celebrity, particularly after *A Taste of Honey* was so successful in the West End. Money was flowing in and Shelagh was pictured in the press lounging in her sloppy joe jumper at home in Salford, with talk of buying an open-top sports car and new clothes and holidays for the family. Her love life naturally came in for a great deal of press speculation, with the various rumours including that of a liaison with the married Irish playwright Brendan Behan, but Shelagh kept her own counsel – only admitting to going out with boys since the age of eleven.

She was taken up by the great and the good: novelist Graham Greene made her a gift of a new typewriter, and fellow playwright John Osborne passed on American offers of an all-expenses-paid trip to New York. Joan Littlewood in her memoirs recalled Shelagh taking it all in her stride, 'giving interviews, considering offers…She was seen in the right pubs coping with the latest drinks and entertaining her hosts with laconic comments in her broad Salford accent.' Her family were naturally astounded at her success, although her father did not live long enough to fully appreciate it. When *A Taste of Honey* was first being performed and money was still tight Shelagh had written to the Arts Council for a bursary to enable her to survive, telling them that her father was an inspector on the Salford corporation buses who was off sick, his only income a war disability pension and his sick pay. He died in July 1958, only a few months after the play's launch. Mother Elsie was very proud of her daughter's achievement and seemingly unfazed by her choice of subject. 'I've read Shelagh's play. It's sexy, but I don't think it's vulgar,' she told reporters at the play's West End premiere, wearing a modest tweed suit bought for the occasion.

Shelagh's younger brother Joe was also present, plus assorted aunts, uncles, cousins and friends from Salford, and after the performance the whole assembly went on for dinner and dancing and a revue at the famous *Talk of the Town* nightclub. The press made fun of the party's 'broad Lancashire tones' and Shelagh herself was even described as like a kennel-maid on her day off, and having puffed at a cigar after wiping the sweat from her brow following eight curtain calls. In fact in the days following the West End premiere there was much harping on her size and 'lumbering' gait, not helped by Shelagh allowing the *Daily Express* to follow her around London taking photographs as she shopped for cigars and ate a pub lunch. Some even made snide references to Shelagh as an angry young *man*.

This was not all Shelagh had to contend with. There was hate mail, some of which she later published: 'What a disgrace not only to the name of THEATRE but to womanhood you are with your dirty clothes and grubby skin and hair. Aren't you ashamed of yourself...By the way, how are your teddy boy friends? Do they carry flick-knives? It would be rather fun if they jab their flick-knives into you one night, it might teach you to improve your tastes and company.' Along with the acclaim came such inevitable criticism, much of it highly personal. In the opinion of Salford-born actor Albert Finney, who had his own problems with fame, Shelagh was actually overwhelmed by the experience. 'The kind of identity crisis she went through,' he said, 'was quite considerable. Much more, I think, *much* more, than mine.'

Back in Salford, opinions on Shelagh were divided. 'Half the town says it's disgusting that I should degrade it,' said Shelagh at the time, continuing that the rest could see she had no intention of degrading anyone. The *Salford City Reporter* took exception to her public comments about being an 11-plus failure with an article entitled 'Shelagh Delaney Accused of Ingratitude to her Teachers'. The editor of the same paper sneered in print that no one could dash off a play in two weeks: it was no more than a sketch, he believed, and Shelagh was lucky that Theatre Workshop had been able to pull off some 'hair-raising stunts' to make it a success. The editor's son then wrote another piece – 'A Taste of Cash for Shelagh But a Kick in the Teeth for Salford' – in which he accused Shelagh of writing about 'half-wits, half-castes, half-tarts, half-pimps and half-homosexuals' and the critics of actually disliking the play but declaring the opposite because they sensed it would be a hit.

Shelagh's forthright mother hit back at the *Salford City Reporter* with a letter entitled by the paper 'Mrs Delaney Says, "Shelagh Loves Salford"', printed on the front page, asking if the writer of the article had never seen slums or a white girl with a coloured baby, and warning that he had better be careful what he said about her daughter Miss Shelagh Delaney or he would find himself in serious trouble. Other letters were written in support of Shelagh and the reality of what she had depicted, and a delegation of eleven angry employees from the Salford Works Department contacted the newspaper to object to their coverage (a 'deliberately manufactured controversy') and to insist that Salford should be proud of Shelagh. But the majority of writers to the paper were critical (despite probably never having seen the play, as it was not performed in Manchester until 1960): 'a nasty piece of sordid filth', 'a British girl spawning a literary monstrosity that bawled vilely as it crawled in the squalor its creator had libellously conceived to be typically Salfordian', 'an execrable play which happens to contain the current jackpot ingredients – vulgarity, perversion, lust, drink, abuse, squalor.' The West End producer of *A Taste of Honey* wrote to the mayor of Salford, inviting him to London to see the play in order to counteract any wrong conceptions he may have picked up from an unsympathetic Manchester press. The mayor's response is not known.

Her mother sent copies of the *Salford City Reporter* to Shelagh when she was staying in London. The scandal in her home town may well have come as a surprise to her but she appeared unrepentant:

I could have laughed when I read some of them. The narrow provincial minds of some of these people amaze me. With great indignation they say that this sort of thing could not happen in Salford and in the same issue of the Reporter there appeared a court story of a woman who had allowed her house where her four children lived to be used as a brothel!

§

The 1961 moodily black-and-white film of *A Taste of Honey* was a box-office winner and international success, leaving lasting impressions of a grim, industrial, but strangely beautiful Salford. It became ranked in the series of iconic Sixties films about the working classes, largely set in the North, which had started in the late 1950s.

The director, Tony Richardson, was desperate to get away from studio-created 'reality' and shatter the suburban, middle-class flavour of current British film, wanting to produce work which highlighted the value and importance of everyday life as lived by ordinary people. Together with playwright John Osborne he had formed a film company to do exactly this, and he bought the film rights to *A Taste of Honey* on its first opening in Stratford East. Shelagh negotiated the deal herself, much to the annoyance of the Theatre Workshop manager who, along with Joan Littlewood, held Shelagh's money in trust for her until she reached the age of majority at twenty-one. He had yet to realise that the young girl from Salford had a mind of her own and was rapidly growing up.

Financial backing for the projected film was hard to find, however – interested American moguls wanted a happy ending with the illegitimate, mixed-race baby either miscarrying or dying and Jo and Helen going on to better things, an idea naturally resisted by realist Tony. He eventually secured funding from the profits made by another iconic working-class film he produced, *Saturday Night and Sunday Morning*, and was able to make this new film exactly the way he wanted. In line with Tony's focus on authenticity this meant shooting on location, with no studio work whatsoever. 'For me,' he had declared, 'studios are death, they are anathema, they are everything I hate'.

There was much press speculation about the choice of actors. The potential American sponsors, bizarrely, had wanted Jo to be played by exquisite Audrey Hepburn, but Tony insisted that he wanted an unknown. John Osborne for some reason told reporters they were looking for an 'ugly' girl, and of course they wanted someone very young: the actresses who had played Jo in the theatre were all far too old to get away with it on camera. The search became intense, with careful scrutiny of myriad photographs plus interviews, auditions and film tests of well over 2,000 hopefuls.

Out of nowhere appeared doe-eyed Rita Tushingham, a teenaged actress from Liverpool whose brother had jokingly told her she was ugly enough to respond to the call. She did not stand out at audition, in fact in Tony's words was much too abrasive to consider seriously, but he remained haunted by the 'little hedgehog'. He sent for her again during the final tests and again felt she was hopeless – but was suddenly convinced on catching a close-up of Rita's 'all-speaking' eyes. The film's backers were horrified, not wanting Rita's unusual looks featuring in publicity. Tony was adamant. Rita exploded on the screen, he would later comment – as far as he was concerned she had the haunting quality of great stars like Marilyn Monroe and Elizabeth Taylor. He also particularly enjoyed using an untried actress, someone who had not already been on screen in dozens of roles. Newcomers were spontaneous and fresh and could be just as professional, he believed.

It was announced, unkindly, that the Ugly Duckling had been found. Rita looked like Donald Duck's sister, the *Daily Mail* commented callously, with her backside waddling when she walked – 'but not, repeat not, in the manner of Miss Marilyn Monroe'. Rita remained unfazed, at least in retrospect. 'I used to look at people and think, well I'm just as good-looking as *them*.' She knew she was a 'different-looking' kind of actress and for her, the fact that she got the role was the main thing. *A Taste of Honey* was to be Rita's road to stardom and many further opportunities in film, including *Dr Zhivago*. Rita took it all in her stride, despite it being her first experience of film acting:

> *I didn't think of the camera. I wasn't intimidated by it. I love the camera and I think because of that I let it in. Some people might be amazing on stage but it's strange – the camera doesn't get anything from them...Ignorance is a wonderful thing. You do things when you're young. Like kids that drive at eighty miles an hour. You just do it without realising what it means.*

The rest of the cast were easier to find, the majority of them similar unknowns, including Paul Danquah as the black sailor Jimmie. Scratchy-voiced comedienne Dora Bryan played Jo's mother Helen – another in the line of loose women frequently portrayed by the actress, who had been specifically requested by Tony Richardson for the role of the 'sluttish mother', as Dora called her. At the time Dora had never seen the play, had no idea who Tony was, and wished she had more information about both the film and Tony's company. She worried about shooting entirely on location and believed the whole project to be extremely precarious, but agreed to go ahead, taking her agent's advice to go for a small lump sum instead of a percentage of the profits – in case there weren't any. Bad advice, as it turned out, with the great success of the film.

Shelagh and Tony collaborated on the script and Shelagh herself appeared very briefly at the beginning of the film as a mostly hidden (but tall) onlooker at a girls' netball game.

Salford, of course, was electrified by the film being made in their midst. The *Salford City Reporter* warned the city's residents to expect to see themselves in the finished work, intent as it was on depicting real people in real settings. This turned out to be particularly true for the local children as Tony included quite a few in his outdoor scenes, he and Shelagh choosing those who looked most scruffy. The action was frequently accompanied by the singing of the children as they played nearby, their songs a sort of lyrical commentary on what was going on that became a key motif. (The film began and ended with the old ditty *The big ship sails on the alley alley oh,* as sung in the original play.) One little girl shown bouncing a ball as Rita and Dora skitter down a flight of stone steps grew up to be MP for Salford: future Labour minister Hazel Blears. 'That film was the most exciting thing that ever happened on Hancock Street,' she remembered. Her proud working-class mother made sure Hazel and her brother were well scrubbed and in their Sunday best to play Tony's street urchins but they were promptly told to go home and get changed into more everyday clothes. He wanted smut on our noses, said Hazel. Three years later, Hazel's Hancock Street was demolished and the residents moved into Salford's new tower blocks; Hazel in later life was grateful that the film of *A Taste of Honey* had captured Salford before the bulldozers piled in – as was Shelagh.

Other local stars in the film were the *S.S. Manchester Shipper* and the *S.S. Manchester Pioneer,* two merchant vessels used as the setting for scenes between Jo and sailor Jimmie which showed glimpses of actors playing drunk crew members – a plot point not made clear to the shipping line beforehand. At the premiere the Manchester

Liners company took space in the programme to point out that it neither approved nor allowed such conduct.

As expected, director Tony Richardson took much of the action away from the four walls of the original production and out into Salford and elsewhere, setting dramatic scenes alongside canals and in front of tenements, pubs and docks. Shelagh herself was often responsible for picking out the locations. The interior scenes in Jo and Helen's bedsits were mostly shot in a derelict house in London, again for a natural, realistic look. Rent for the house cost only £20 a week, in comparison to the £2000 they would have paid for studio space, but filming on location in this way was then seen as audacious and even foolhardy. Tony's intention was to reach for the basic truthfulness and naturalness of Shelagh's work, which he believed had been obscured by the razzamatazz of the theatre production, but at the same time to present its poetry, her characters' ability to experience warmth and romance in their bleak environment.

Once Rita Tushingham had been found to play the central role, the making of the film went swimmingly: 'a lovefest with both crew and actors', according to Tony, an experience totally without the constraints imposed by studio work. The naturalistic way they shot the film was at the mercy of real life, he commented. 'If it's raining we don't wait for the sun to come out, we just play the scene in the rain. If there's a wind blowing which gets the leading actress's hair untidy, we shoot her looking untidy. Of course if we had a big female star in the film we couldn't do this...we haven't the time or the inclination to bother about obtaining the most flattering shots.' Such an attitude, standard enough now, was highly unorthodox at the time. The result was radical and stunning, due in the main to the film's brilliant and inspired camerawork.

Given the approach to filming, some effects were a matter of chance, such as the scene when a gloomy Jo and Geof are talking under a railway viaduct and the sun bursts through just as the two come to the point in the screenplay where they cheer up and run joyfully through the arch. Other effects were carefully calculated by the talented director of photography Walter Lassally, who made highly effective use of lightweight, easily manoeuvred cameras when out on location and flew in the face of convention with his radical use of differing types of film stock for indoor and outdoor work. Grimy, industrial Salford became a place of eerie, almost unearthly beauty, with the star of the film arguably the city just as much as the characters.

Rita Tushingham and the other actors played their roles superbly, aided by director Tony's knack of wringing depths of meaning out of them with largely silent close-ups. Tony helped Rita over the difficult bits, she recalled. One of the trickiest was learning to act as though the growing baby had kicked her:

That's pretty hard to do if you've never had a baby. Learning to walk like a pregnant woman was not easy either. I didn't exactly go around staring at them, but whenever I saw one I'd try to notice how they walk.

Rita, who was in the very early stages of her acting career and had done little more than playing the hind legs of a horse for Liverpool Repertory – literally – had been astonished when she landed the role of Jo. After Tony Richardson rang her up to confirm she was to play the starring role, she spent some time after the call asking herself whether he had actually said 'You've got the part' or 'You *haven't* got the part.' Tony had needed to fight to keep her: the financial people still wanted a known actress and needed persuading, which was to lead to a delay in filming.

Rita had enjoyed reading the play, recognising Shelagh's freedom of spirit and the fresh air she brought into the theatre, and the way she had written about what she saw around her. But she did not go and see it performed, wanting to avoid inadvertently copying the interpretation of another actress. She had her own take: Jo was unloved but wanting to be loved, Rita thought, and played it accordingly. She wore no makeup for the film, something that was later commented on by reviewers, along with the many references to her wonderfully expressive eyes. She was perfectly happy with the unmade-up look, despite the shock of such a raw effect after the heavily painted actresses of what she called the chocolate box 1950s.

During the shooting she became great friends with Paul Danquah playing sailor Jimmie, with whom in the film she improvises a little dance while he pretends to play the bongo; they also exchanged what Rita thought was the first interracial kiss in British cinema. (While they were walking through Soho together one day, a passer-by yelled out 'Blacks and whites don't mix!' Paul shouted back, 'Don't worry! She's only been on holiday and got a tan.')

The film keeps more or less to the script of the play although adding a few extra scenes and supplying more backstory, such as how Jo and Geof first meet – making their friendship more authentic and believable – and tying up loose ends for a tighter feel. There is one major departure. Jo's mother Helen is not the distant, occasionally cold figure of the play who has repeatedly left her young daughter alone every Christmas to go off with some man – and asks her daughter 'Have I ever laid claim to being a proper mother?' when asked to cook a meal like one – but a scattier, warmer version with her daughter's interests essentially at heart. The ending leaves the relationship between mother and daughter far more positive than in the original, with Helen returning to be a support to her pregnant daughter (as Murray Melvin again playing Geof walks away, almost stealing the show).

Despite this fairly upbeat conclusion, however, the film version of *A Taste of Honey*, and its perhaps heavy-handed focus on grim reality, leaves a much bleaker and more defeated impression than the play with all its exuberant wit, comic effects and jazz music. What Tony Richardson called the 'forcedly jolly' nature of Shelagh's play, as produced by Joan Littlewood and Theatre Workshop, was deliberately jettisoned.

The British Board of Film Censors gave the film an 'X' because of Jo's youth and pregnancy, the ripe language and, of course, the overtly homosexual Geof. The absolute essentials stipulated were that Jo not be too young in appearance – the actress should be at least sixteen – and Geof not too 'sissy' or 'an exaggerated nancy boy'. The fact that Jo's seaman lover was black was of no particular consequence, it was stated.

It was another resounding success, winning British Film Academy Awards for Best British Film, Best British Screenplay, Best British Actress (Dora) and Most Promising Newcomer (Rita). Shelagh and Tony shared the scriptwriting award – the first time a woman had ever won it – and gained a Writers' Guild of Great Britain award into the bargain. In the States, in spite of dealing with topics not usually featuring in that country's more Puritan film industry, *A Taste of Honey* secured Rita a 1963 Golden Globe award for Most Promising Female Newcomer and for Tony Richardson, a nomination for the 1963 Directors Guild of America award. Profits were well in excess of the paltry £120,000 it had cost to make.

British critics saluted the authentically realised environment, the 'shabby streets and wet pavements, the school playgrounds, the public monuments and the rubbish-strewn canals', but rightly saw more in the film than just a credible kitchen sink drama. They recognised the poetry of Tony's vision and that of the film's director of photography Walter Lassally, who had worked hard to imbue *A Taste of Honey* with atmosphere and lyricism. The *Daily Herald* wrote that it fulfilled Tony's 'poetic promise', and for many critics the film far surpassed the theatre production and indeed even Shelagh's original itself, the play's weaknesses of plot and structure still apparent in the film and the excessive realism actually serving to point up the thinness of the material. Rita had 'the sort of face and quality,' said critic Penelope Gilliat, 'that one has pined for through all the years of Surrey-rose ingenues'. There was general acclaim, the *Sunday Times* applauding the work's 'sensitive desolate images'. It was hard to imagine that it had ever been anything but a film, wrote the *Spectator*. Abroad, the *Australian Women's Weekly* hailed the film's devastatingly comic candour and delicate handling of a 'sordid theme' – dynamic, was the verdict. For Canadian magazine *Maclean's* Rita was a 'radiant little ugly duckling', the film funny and angry and better than the original play, even if its unblinking scrutiny of human frailties proved offensive to some viewers.

Tony no doubt enjoyed the accolades, although Rita Tushingham was later to comment that he didn't 'give a fuck if it was popular [with the critics]...he wanted to make something for the ordinary working class, he had that sense of purpose'. Shelagh reportedly agreed with this view.

Rita and Murray also won Best Actress and Actor awards at the 1962 Cannes Film Festival – in Rita's case at the insistence of celebrated French director François Truffaut, according to his own account. Both Dora and Rita were invited to the festival and greatly enjoyed themselves, although bemused at having to mix with people on the business side of films at all the dinners and parties. The wives were all extremely glamorous, remembered Dora, attired in minks and jewellery and gorgeous dresses. She was grateful for her one single mink stole and Rita looked stylish in a pretty woollen one, but both were aware they offered little competition either to the wives or the glamour girls on the beach, who shocked Dora by going topless. 'Look at her!' Rita remembered Dora saying. 'Why's she doing *that*.' Despite the award the two often went unrecognised: they just did not look like film stars, said Rita. They were refused entry to the reception after the film's premiere and had to stand outside a window, waving and trying to attract attention, until famous film critic Alexander Walker spotted them and got them in. (Perhaps doing so as a sort of apology, as he had been less than flattering about Rita in his review: 'A crow's nest of hair, a ski-tip nose, a mouth you could fit a saucer into – a cup and saucer when it is open – and eyes that have a mongrel dogginess in their depths.')

Neither was very sophisticated at the time, by their own admission, although the older and more experienced actress Dora inevitably more so than Rita. At one particularly smart dinner there was a selection of crudités on the table, which Rita promptly complained about because the vegetables weren't cooked, and then compounded her faux pas by asking the disdainful waiters for Coke instead of wine. To the delight of the press both began to play up to the image of no-nonsense Lancashire women, deliberately giving the reporters some good copy by bemoaning the lack of fish and chips. Asked her opinion of a gourmet onion dish Dora roundly declared 'They cook onions here the way we in Lancashire use them to cure colds!' Neither, of course, was as naïve as they were pretending to be. Rita later went to America to promote the film and appeared on several popular talk shows.

The film was controversial for the period – and was banned in a number of countries because of its subject matter – but is now universally recognised as a classic. Film historians have nevertheless pointed to the film's beautifying of squalor and the fact that the view taken of the North was a middle-class one which saw the landscape and the people as somehow alien, even threatening, with the beauty of the film only serving to distance the viewer from the problems of the characters. Not everyone would agree, especially with Rita Tushingham's talented performance eliciting such sympathy from the viewer. (Rita, like Shelagh, had to put up with London critics assuming that her background mirrored that of her character Jo, when in fact her father owned a grocery shop and was a Conservative councillor, and Shelagh's family were perfectly respectable.)

The original stage performers of *A Taste of Honey* were somewhat sniffy about the film version. It was hard to watch other people delivering lines that she had only thrown in in the first place, said Avis Bunnage, and Joan Littlewood agreed that Dora Bryan spoke lines the company had merely improvised as if they were 'great literary products'. The film's music was 'terribly syrupy', commented the jazz band's trumpet player. As for Shelagh, she was not very happy with the film. Rita was too 'sweet' for the role of spiky Jo, she always thought, but had trusted to Tony Richardson's judgement in casting her. In the end she had not been that involved in the actual making of the film, being away in New York in connection with the production of her play there, and with Shelagh not present Tony had moved the focus away from the mother and daughter relationship and made Jo more the centre.

§

To publicise her second play Shelagh was persuaded to smarten herself up, relinquishing her usual jeans and jumper and reluctantly visiting a top London designer, where she bought an expensive suit with tapered skirt but rejected a beaver-lined coat because of her belief (much ahead of her time) that it was 'unwholesome' to wear dead animals. The makeover was not to last. Shelagh had already made clear in interviews that she felt stifled in smart clothes and preferred dressing comfortably, her fisherman's sweaters and paint-spattered jeans duly commented on by the reporters. Fashion, she said, was 'followed slavishly by women who have too much time on their hands, too much money and too little imagination'. If she wore jewellery she preferred big, artificial items, chunky bangles and earrings that looked like 'toned-down stage effects'.

In further publicity efforts she was also the subject of a famous Ken Russell documentary for the BBC, *Shelagh Delaney's Salford*, in which she appeared running with her dog by the canal, slicing bread for tea at the family home and standing at the docks admitting to an abiding love of her 'dying' home city, which was then in the process of being demolished and rebuilt. Her regret for the old Salford being torn down, and pity for the many being rehoused in strange modern flats and living without much hope for the future, are palpable. As for herself, said Shelagh, she could never live all her life in Salford: she was too restless a person and always would be. Salford, unsurprisingly, was again indignant at Shelagh's criticisms of both the old and the new Salford, and at Ken Russell's focus on smoke and grime and dirty river.

Her second (or possibly third) play *The Lion in Love* was rejected by Joan Littlewood at Theatre Workshop as unappealing and even more shapeless than the first script ('She had learned nothing,' Joan wrote in her memoirs). Shelagh therefore turned elsewhere. The play, a domestic drama once more set in Salford, made its debut in

Coventry before going on tour with the aim of ending up in the West End. But notices were bad, many critics unimpressed by the lack of any real action or resolution, although again appreciative of the lively dialogue. To herald the play's Manchester opening Shelagh gave a press conference, appearing this time in a grubby white mac and hastily tied scarf to parry the usual questions about her dress sense and love life. She was the nearest the locals had to a home-grown Garbo but without the looks, a mean *Guardian* journalist commented, adding that she possessed the same talent for creating racy headlines.

The play folded after losing money on tour and then failing to find a theatre willing to put it on in the West End. Shelagh made the best of it, at least for public consumption, and professed to be getting on with yet another play while dividing her time between London and Salford. *The Lion in Love* did eventually find a theatre in London but closed after twenty-eight performances (not actually a bad run), still eliciting much criticism although gaining support from the likes of John Osborne. Shelagh made little of this failure, apart from an apparently angry rant in a *Daily Mail* interview about the Lord Chamberlain's office making her take the word 'bugger' out of the script, which she defended as being almost a term of endearment among Northerners. She also lit into the hypocrisy of audiences who roared their heads off at sly innuendoes but were aghast at honest-to-goodness sex. 'Miss Delaney savagely ground out her umpteenth cigarette and immediately lit another,' wrote the reporter.

She continued to believe in the play – which in fact won a few awards – and eventually took it to America. Unfortunately this time the play closed after only six showings and was never further performed. Shelagh did not write again for the stage for twenty years.

However, seemingly undaunted, she remained a popular guest on TV and radio and even in demand for trips abroad. At the same time she became more overtly political (and was already a subject of interest to MI5, who had started a file on her in connection with her work with radical Joan Littlewood). She talked about the class system on BBC radio along with writers Alan Sillitoe and Dennis Potter, and took part in an anti-nuclear sit-down demonstration in Trafalgar Square which led to her arrest and that of many others including John Osborne and actress Vanessa Redgrave. (As they left the magistrates' court the following morning, after each being fined two pounds, Vanessa linked arms with Shelagh and declared her readiness to go to prison if necessary – Shelagh, though, stating that she would prefer not to enter any more police stations.) A couple of years later she joined a group of playwrights refusing to allow their work to be performed in any theatre in apartheid South Africa which excluded black people.

There was a failed attempt to start up a 'community theatre' in Salford, a type of theatre which would also act as a kind of community centre. Shelagh wanted to see plays put on about the reality of Salford lives, although not exclusively. But there was local resistance to the idea, apparently with its roots in the animosity Shelagh's work had aroused in Salfordians in tandem with the suspicion that radical, commie-type thinking lay behind the plan. There seemed to be 'a strong feeling against Shelagh Delaney from many people,' commented the estate agent engaged to search for suitable premises for the project. It came to nothing.

§

In March 1964 Shelagh gave birth to a daughter, Charlotte Jo Delaney, in a private nursing home in Paddington. The baby's father was married American comedy writer and talent agent Harvey Orkin, twenty years older than Shelagh, who lived in the US. A permanent liaison was never on the cards. He may well have been the love of her life, a close friend of Shelagh's was later to observe, but even had he been free it was doubtful that the independent Shelagh would ever have married him. They continued a secret relationship until his brain tumour death at the early age of fifty-seven, the news coming as a great shock to Shelagh as his family were not aware of their relationship and had not made his illness generally known.

Shelagh had been surprised but thrilled by the pregnancy, friends recalled. She returned with new daughter Charlotte to the London flat she shared with a friend, supported by her mother who had come to help. Journalists were waiting for her and remained camped outside the door and outside the flats so that she was unable to leave. There was even a story that, desperate for a photo of Shelagh with the baby, journalists set off a fire alarm in the building in the hope that everyone would run out. But apart from a brief exchange with a *Daily Express* reporter soon after the birth, Shelagh did not disclose anything about either the father or her marital status. Visiting friends found her much distressed by the press attention; she had been very hurt over the years by some of their comments, especially in regards to her family. She did not talk to the media again for over a decade. Fame, it seemed, was not for Shelagh.

She continued to write, in 1963 producing a mostly ignored semi-autobiographical collection of prose pieces and later co-writing a script based on one of them for a short, very satirical film – luckily for the still locally unpopular Shelagh, mostly unshown – about a bus tour of what is clearly Manchester and Salford. This was *The White Bus*, in which a girl loosely based on Shelagh is visiting her home town and takes the tour. Arthur Lowe of later *Dad's Army* fame plays the mayor showing some foreign dignitaries around the city, and Anthony Hopkins makes his film debut in a minor role. (The film is sometimes cited as the inspiration for the Beatles' *Magical Mystery Tour*, issued that same year, although the Beatles themselves mentioned different influences.) Despite often being dismissed as a one-hit wonder, Shelagh was to remain a successful (if intermittent) author, writing for the gritty TV police series *Z Cars* and co-scripting the film *Charlie Bubbles* with actor and fellow Salfordian Albert Finney, star of the film. The plot, devised by Shelagh, revolved around a successful writer returning to Manchester and Salford, where he meets with barely concealed malice from the envious townspeople and feels disconnected from his working-class roots. She also wrote popular and critically acclaimed plays for television (frequently featuring women for whom marriage and motherhood were not the whole story of their lives) and the screenplay for the very successful film *Dance with a Stranger*, about the last woman to be hanged in Britain. In 1985, finally respectable, she was made a fellow of the Royal Society of Literature. All of this body of work, and recognition, was a cause of great pride to Shelagh. She was never merely the precocious author of *A Taste of Honey*, as the press would always have her.

Salford ceased to be the backdrop of all her work, although she returned to the subject in the last decade of her life with radio scripts reflecting on the city's destruction. A shabby and soulless shopping centre now stood in place of the lively old market; her home town had had its heart pulled out, she wrote. In 2001 she tried, but failed, to avert the demolition of the old Ambassador Cinema where Violet Carson, Ena Sharples in *Coronation Street*, had once played the piano to accompany the silent films.

She continued to live her life against the stereotype, a successful single mother, creative writer and friend – but one who staunchly maintained her independence. There were further relationships, including possibly a female lover, and some musing over whether she was bisexual, although according to her daughter she was always sexually attracted to men. Shelagh remained fiercely private about such matters.

There were seemingly few regrets. 'I earned a lot of money, I spent it all. I loved the parties, I loved the cocktails,' she reminisced to a confidant. In her later years, after a dwindling income no longer allowed a home in London, she lived by herself in a tiny, isolated cottage in Yorkshire where she made new friends but sometimes felt lonely. She still suffered intermittent self-consciousness about her height, on one occasion even storming out of a supermarket because she thought the assistants were making remarks about how tall she was. Shelagh died of cancer and heart failure in 2011, aged seventy-two, at the home of her playwright daughter Charlotte – a writer and a rebel like her mother – whom as a child she had frequently taken to visit Salford, the town she once described as like 'a terrible drug' that she couldn't get away from.

Shelagh specifically bequeathed to Charlotte the task of granting or refusing permission to stage *A Taste of Honey*, a request that Shelagh herself had more often than not rejected, wanting to be thought of as more than just its author and not enjoying the attention it still brought. When she was dying she told Charlotte she was glad to be leaving it behind.

Asked what her mother was really like, Charlotte replied:

She was a good friend, loyal, a fabulous grandma. She was always playful – she never lost that – and she never had her head turned by fame, not even after Katharine Hepburn took her for a drive in Spencer Tracy's car. She was a socialist. She could talk to anyone, no matter who they were: Ringo Starr, or her mum's neighbour. She was infuriating, she was adventurous…she was a renegade.

After her death tributes poured in from around the world, all of them reflecting on the radical contribution made by *A Taste of Honey* to British theatre.

§

A Taste of Honey, like *Look Back in Anger*, was ultimately categorised as a 'kitchen sink' play, a drama depicting realistic scenes of usually Northern working-class life.

With time the final version of the play was hailed as possibly the first feminist piece of British theatre: in the words of author Jeanette Winterson, a work with two fabulous female roles where the women are not merely adjuncts. The women are indeed central, the male characters marginal, and the way the women are depicted certainly suggests evolving ideas about female reality before such ideas were mainstream – that women have strength and character, that not all women have the maternal instinct, and that motherhood can be unwelcome and the idea of breastfeeding abhorrent. 'I'm not having a little animal nibbling away at me,' says Jo, 'it's cannibalistic'.

It has also been recognised as an early beacon of racial tolerance and for its handling of homosexuality, up until then only referred to obliquely on the stage because of censorship. Some months after the play came out the ban on depicting homosexual subjects on the stage was partially removed, and, following Shelagh's death in 2011, critic Nicholas de Jongh commented that her treatment of the subject and the favourable critical and public response to *A Taste of Honey* may well have played a significant role in persuading the Lord Chamberlain to lift the ban. Her sympathetic portrayal of young, gay Geof was groundbreaking, he declared, and Shelagh Delaney ought to rank as a gay heroine. Writer Colin MacInnes declared *A Taste of Honey* to be the first English play he had ever seen in which 'a coloured man, and a queer boy, are presented as natural characters, factually without a nudge or shudder'. The actor Murray Melvin, who played the part of Geof in both play and film, agreed. He was always proud that he played the character with dignity and not as a mincing caricature – claiming that he refused director Tony Richardson's instructions to come out of a shop swinging his hips:

I played a gay person not as a figure of fun – which was the norm for gay characters in 1957, but as a character with dignity.

But the question often asked is how much *A Taste of Honey* was actually Shelagh's own work. Was the play as written by Shelagh really such a striking piece and such a beacon for feminism, gay rights and racial tolerance? Joan Littlewood always freely admitted that she made substantial changes to the original script, although she was too experienced a director to have accepted a play with absolutely no merit. That such changes were made was confirmed by many of those involved in the initial production.

However, Frances Cuka, the actress who first played Jo on stage, insisted that, despite the reworking, scene-cutting and improvisation instigated by Joan, the play remained essentially as it initially arrived. It had needed 'a heck of a cut to it' but the best bits, she said, were Shelagh's. This is borne out by a comparison of Shelagh's original (badly spelt) script, now held in the British Library, and the final version as performed on stage. The fundamentals of the play are indeed all there: the sarcasm, the witty one-liners, the bleak plot and the unforgettable characters – including most fundamentally of all, the fully formed character of Jo. That first script also demonstrates Shelagh's clever intertwining of everyday Lancashire dialogue with the rhythms of both serious and popular theatre, including music hall, with the characters snapping and wisecracking at each other like a comedy double act. It shows, too, that Shelagh's focus was always on the women. Right from the start male characters are not at the heart of the play but at its periphery, and this aspect of the play, later greeted as revolutionary, was firmly present in her original work. Jo and her mother are strong, uncompromising characters who accept, and even relish, the prospect of a life without men: they are just not essential.

As for Shelagh being a gay heroine, however, there are at least some question marks. She acceded to the Lord Chamberlain's requests to tone down the references to homosexuality – as was necessary to get the play performed at all – but in addition there are signs of homophobia and ignorance in Shelagh's original script

51

such as a reference from Jo to 'simpering pansified little freaks' and a ludicrous explanation of how Geof came to prefer men. But all the same, Geof is never a gay caricature. He is always sympathetically and roundly depicted, if somewhat ambivalent in his sexuality, and this was truly radical for the times. Since the film, actor Murray Melvin has many times been approached by young people thanking him for playing the part and saying it had changed their lives: 'You made it possible for me.' He had been the start of gay pride, Murray believed.

The changes that *were* made at Theatre Workshop were often sensible tweaks which cut out the worst of the juvenilia and tightened up the action and characterisation. Shelagh's first typescript was darker, for instance: Jo talks about wanting to commit suicide (and claiming to have tried to do so) by taking pills or gassing, hanging, stabbing or drowning herself, and wanting to kill her infant by tying a brick around its neck and drowning it. Nearly all of this was removed – probably because it came across as over the top, not very credible – and Jo is left with the single eruption that she would bash the baby's brains out. (The celebrated line that followed this, that she didn't want to be a mother, didn't want to be a woman, was in fact *added* by Theatre Workshop.) In the first version Jo also tries to grab a knife on going into labour – again, cut from the final version. Other changes were the tweaking of Helen's lover Peter to become a nastier piece of work than Shelagh's original more sympathetic conception, and an alteration to the ending, with an even more selfish Helen not clearly intending to come back to help Jo in her hour of need. The play as a result of all these amendments was far less teenagerish, far more effective. But there can be no doubt: despite the alterations, the fundamentals of *A Taste of Honey* are all Shelagh's.

On the subject of race, *A Taste of Honey* as first written by Shelagh is almost wholly devoid of prejudice – again, highly unusual for the era. But changes made in this regard present a murky picture. When the play transferred to the West End, Joan Littlewood resisted efforts to have it recast with celebrities but did make additional changes to the dialogue, in particular where race was concerned. In Shelagh's original Geof reveals very matter-of-factly to Helen that the coming baby may be black, and the news is accepted by Helen seemingly in the same spirit, with the colour of the father apparently having little import for either of them. These lines were changed by Joan to be a little stronger in the first production – and then made even stronger for the West End:

JO: *My baby may be black.*

HELEN: *You filthy bitch!*

JO: *I knew you'd say that...Where are you going?*

HELEN: *To get myself a drink. Black! A picanniny! A bloody chocolate drop! Oh, my God! Can you see me wheeling a pram with a – I'll have to have a drink.*

A Taste of Honey, Shelagh Delaney, 1958

The lines are intentionally more shocking, a disservice to the original conception of the play as a whole and to the character of Helen, who was never envisaged in this way by Shelagh. Jo (herself wholly without prejudice) explicitly states in the original that whatever Helen is, she is no racist, and this appears to be the case, despite one use of a racial epithet which is probably meant only jokingly and which Geof objects to. Shelagh later regretted these changes by Joan and revised them for the production of her play on Broadway in 1960.

§

Today, the play's subject matter is less shocking to modern tastes but continues to resonate: teenagers still get pregnant, mixed-race babies still arrive, people continue to be gay or trapped in poverty. Above all, of course, it is Shelagh's wit and passion and hope for the future that maintain their grip. *A Taste of Honey* is still performed all over the world, on stage and on television, and has even been remade as a foreign film. The script has featured on school curricula and both play and film have been subjected to repeated analysis.

Cultural reverberations have likewise echoed down the years. Manchester pop star Morrissey, of The Smiths, was massively influenced by Shelagh's writing: 'the sagging-roof poetry of Shelagh Delaney's rag-and-bone plays says *something* to me about my life,' he declared in his autobiography. He, too, identified with society's marginals and was deeply interested in the effects of poverty; in plays like *A Taste of Honey*, he observed, for the first time people were allowed regional accents and to be truthful and honest about their situation. As far as Morrissey was concerned the film version was 'virtually the only important thing in British film in the 1960s'; he would boast of being able to recite the script word-for-word. He claimed that at least fifty percent of his reason for writing was down to Shelagh, admitting that he overdid it and that it took a long time to shed her influence. (His obsession even extended somewhat to *Taste of Honey* star Dora Bryan, whom he once invited to his London flat for a discussion of her old black-and-white films, regaling the bemused actress – who had never heard of him – with rosehip tea and Healthy Life biscuits.) Words from Shelagh's plays appeared in the Smiths' very first single, *Hand in Glove*, in 1983, while Rita Tushingham in her role as Jo was featured on the sleeve of a collaborative cover version by 1960s singer Sandie Shaw the following year.

More of Shelagh's work was to feature in subsequent Smiths songs such as *This Night Has Opened My Eyes* (Geof's line 'The dream's gone, but the baby's real enough') and *Reel Around the Fountain* (sailor Jimmie's line 'I dreamt about you last night. Fell out of bed twice'); and her face appeared on the single *Girlfriend In A Coma* and on the best-selling Smiths compilation album *Louder Than Bombs*, Morrissey's favourite Smiths sleeve. She had a 'strange sexiness about her,' said Morrissey, 'even with her overcoat on.'

Others, too, came under the Shelagh Delaney spell, most notably future *Coronation Street* scriptwriter Tony Warren – prompting some to wonder if Helen was possibly the model for the series' rackety character Elsie Tanner. Indeed Shelagh's greatest influence, the *Sunday Times* once argued, was surely on television soap operas 'about lower-class people shouting at each other'. Tony tried to inveigle Shelagh into working on Corrie but she deemed the soap too cosy and nostalgic. 'Caps and muffler,' she said. 'That's all it is: caps and muffler.'

Inevitably, *A Taste of Honey* is now better known as the film than as the play. For all its deliberate or accidental departures from Shelagh's original intentions it is the film, with its starkly beautiful capture of Salford, the mesmerising quality of Rita Tushingham's round-eyed gaze, and the nostalgia it evokes for a lost world of rainswept, cobbled streets that remain in the memory.

Salford has long forgiven Shelagh and now fully embraces her, with a Shelagh Delaney Day instituted by Salford Arts Theatre and a block of affordable flats named 'Delaney Heights' after the city's most rebellious daughter. There is also a plaque on her former family home, unveiled by her old friend Harold Riley in 2014.

Photo licensed under
CC BY-NC-SA 2.0

He was very honoured to be unveiling the plaque for Shelagh, said the artist:

She was one of the people in my life that I loved very much...Shelagh was always very forthright, she was a person with great charisma and she was beautiful. The most interesting thing about her, more than anything else, was the warmth inside her. And more than anything else, she shouldn't be forgotten.

§

Was Shelagh actually angry when she wrote *A Taste of Honey*? She was often perceived so. 'If there's anything worse than an Angry Young Man it's an Angry Young Woman,' the *Daily Mail* declared after the opening night. Playwright Noel Coward described her play as a 'squalid little piece about squalid and unattractive people...written by an angry young lady of nineteen', while in America, the *New York Mirror* deemed her 'a snarling, cynical young Englishwoman' who had written 'an ode to misery'. She could certainly come across that way. Murray Melvin described her as practically born angry. When she was advised against buying a sports car by the manager of Theatre Workshop she made her fury fairly evident in a letter:

I've never liked being told what to do and I've no intentions of starting to like it now. You have no right whatsoever to order me about like some Industrial Revolution employer. I'm not going to crawl round people's backsides like some suckholing spineless fly. I've been offered a lot of money for the film rights of my play and I want that car.

(When she turned twenty-one and finally had management of her own money, Shelagh went ahead and bought the car – despite the fact that she couldn't drive. She subsequently gave it to her brother.)

But in fact Shelagh hated the 'Angry Young Woman' label and thought her play more about resilience in the face of what life can throw at you:

No one in my play despairs. Like the majority of people they take in their stride whatever happens to them and remain cheerful.

It is true that Jo does not appear as angry about her lot as the central character in John Osborne's *Look Back in Anger* (although angrier than her mother Helen); rather, she accepts what occurs and takes responsibility for it. Nevertheless, threads of anger do make themselves felt throughout the play: about the way the working class were treated, about how men treat women, and how for women marriage and motherhood were never everything and yet perforce shaped their existence. Shelagh was always to reject the angry tag, however. Interviewed on TV when the play first appeared, she pointed out that anybody under thirty was an angry young man or woman to those over forty who once thought they might do something but then didn't. She was no fan of *Look Back in Anger*, which she described as 'bloody awful, as a whole' (despite Osborne standing up for Shelagh, whose play to him was an acutely sensitive portrayal of a group of warm, immediately recognisable people). She would continue to refute the label. She had never been 'an angry young woman – what have I got to be angry about?'

Author Jeanette Winterson has argued that Shelagh wasn't angry but restless (a favourite word of Shelagh's) and in fact oddly full of optimism, depicting a Northern spirit with unselfpitying toughness which left room for humour. For Jeanette her language was fantastic:

muscular, taut, feisty, strong. In her view Shelagh took ordinary lives and gave them operatic value, so that instead of patronising the North, her play said 'We're here' but also, 'we're *big*'. And the great thing about *A Taste of Honey* was that nobody was a victim. It was real people fighting for their lives – but doing it with some dignity and grandeur.

Beyond that, said Jeanette, Shelagh inspired, bestowing a sense of ambition and what can be achieved. She was a beacon for women writers to come:

Women all over the world are writing plays and films now – women are writing plays and films about women. Shelagh Delaney deserves a major re-write in all those histories of post-war drama because Shelagh Delaney is the start of the possible.

Shelagh, by Harold Riley

The L-Shaped Room

Lynne Reid Banks

My room was five flights up in one of those gone-to-seed houses in Fulham, all dark brown paper inside and peeling paint outside. On every second landing was a chipped sink with one tap and an old ink-written notice which said 'Don't Leave Tap Driping'. The landing lights were the sort that go out before you can reach the next one. There were a couple of prostitutes in the basement; the landlady had been quite open about them. She'd pointed out that there was even an advantage to having them there, namely that nobody asked questions about anybody. She dropped her eyes as she said that. Not out of modesty. She was looking to see if I were pregnant. Just because you don't ask questions, her look said, it doesn't mean you're not curious. But I had only been pregnant a month, so of course there was nothing to see.

The L-Shaped Room, Lynne Reid Banks, 1960

§

When *The L-Shaped Room* became an immediate bestseller in 1960 its author, TV journalist Lynne Reid Banks, was utterly astonished. But her story of a pregnant single woman who resolves to keep her child – in what were then very unforgiving times – turned out to be a perennial classic, with some readers even well into the next century placing it third on a list of ten books they would most like to have on a desert island. It appeared to resonate everywhere, and it was to dawn on Lynne over the years that, although she never received any letters from readers to whom it had really happened, many had nevertheless found reading her book a deeply personal and unforgettable experience.

Lynne was born in London in 1929, the only child of Scottish doctor James and beautiful former actress Pat. Her father, a GP in a poor area of Hammersmith in

London, struggled with lifelong debt inherited from his father's original purchase of the practice. Her Irish mother sent her daughter at the age of nine to a Catholic boarding school following criticisms that Lynne was a spoilt only child. When Lynne was then desperately homesick, Pat solved the problem by moving into a cottage in the school grounds and helping out at the school.

During World War II the resourceful Pat took Lynne and a boy cousin to Canada, to wait it out in safety in a little house on the wrong side of the tracks in the growing city of Saskatoon, Saskatchewan. Because she had her mother with her Lynne was perfectly happy as an evacuee, despite being poor and unable to afford fashionable clothes as she grew into a teenager. She had little conception of what war actually meant until the end of hostilities in 1945 and her return to England, aged fifteen. Finding London in ruins and learning what had been happening to the rest of the family left Lynne in shock and feeling like a deserter; to make matters worse, neither her own nor her mother's relationship with her abandoned father ever truly recovered. She also had no idea of the horrors experienced by the Jewish population in Europe, and seeing newsreels of Belsen and Auschwitz so affected her that she became sympathetic to all things Jewish and fascinated by the new state of Israel. She was to remain so for all of her adult life.

On a lighter note, the returning Lynne was aghast at the old-fashioned ways of other girls her age. In Canada she had worn rolled-up jeans with sloppy joe jumpers, danced to the Hit Parade on the jukebox and mooned over Frank Sinatra. In England she found girls who had never heard of Frank, wore no makeup, and were still in the sashed, puff-sleeved crêpe dresses chosen by their mothers. Worst of all, there was no dating or what she called 'smooching'.

British teenagers soon caught up with their transatlantic contemporaries but to start with Lynne felt far more grown-up, and somewhat racy in comparison.

On completing her education she decided to become an actress like her mother, who had always regretted dutifully giving up her acting career to become the wife of a doctor. After some secretarial training she attended London's Italia Conti drama school and then the prestigious Royal Academy of Dramatic Art (RADA), afterwards embarking on a five-year slog in acting companies performing up and down the country. This was to be the proving ground for Lynne as a writer: as she acted she also began to write short stories – never published – and to write plays. By the age of twenty-four she was appearing in her own Yorkshire comedy *It Never Rains*, which she wrote in ten days when stuck in bed with flu.

It was during Lynne's acting period that she first encountered the original 'Angry Young Man' John Osborne, at that point also an actor, and found herself embroiled in his private affairs. She was then about twenty, as was John, and fresh from drama school. Both were working for the same penniless travelling theatre group. John disliked the well-spoken Lynne on sight, thinking her snooty, a 'professional virgin' and, in terms of any sexual attraction for John, 'unspeakable'. To his annoyance, she was prone to casting herself in the role of chaperone to the other two young girls in the company in case he tried it on with them. She and John did not get on, was Lynne's politer observation about the working-class young actor. 'It was a class thing...' She also commented that his acting left a lot to be desired (true, from all accounts), especially if he disliked a play they were performing. Their paths diverged but some time later, when John Osborne was on the point of marrying Lynne's former RADA contemporary Pamela Lane, Lynne was asked by Pamela's parents for help in persuading their daughter against the marriage. Mrs Lane begged Lynne to go and convince Pamela that John was homosexual. She agreed, and turned up one evening at the theatre where John and Pamela were working – 'to my HORROR,' said John. 'We looked at each other with open loathing.' Whatever Lynne may have said, however, Pamela was clearly not convinced and the marriage went ahead. In her more mature years Lynne was not proud of her role in this incident and admitted that she knew her accusation was false, even though making some sort of case out of once being startled to see Osborne in a play wearing very heavy makeup which included green eyeshadow.

John got his revenge on Lynne, at least according to him. At a party Lynne gave after they both became well known, he offered her a sandwich into which he claimed to have inserted a used condom. 'The unbelieving repulsion on her face,' John exulted, 'the prig struck by lightning...'

Lynne had enjoyed her acting years (although in John Osborne's opinion disapproving of the dissolute way of life) but eventually saw that she was never really going to succeed on the stage – in fact 'failed dismally', in her own words. When her father died suddenly, apparently leaving her mother without financial support, Lynne realised she needed more regular employment and in 1954 put acting behind her. She became a research secretary to the Jewish writer Wolf Mankowitz, but continued writing plays until her ambitions suffered a serious blow when *It Never Rains* was shown on BBC television and slammed by the critics. 'It Never Rains But

65

It Bores' was the title of one review (incredibly, written by a friend of hers). She decided to take another path.

By the middle of the decade she was breaking ground as one of the first female television reporters in Britain, working at the newly founded Independent Television News (ITN), which was keen to promote itself as less stuffy and hidebound than the BBC. Together with another pioneer 'girl reporter', the celebrated Barbara Mandell (not to be confused with American singer Barbara Mandrell), she was out on the streets conducting interviews with members of the public – the first instance of 'vox pop' in the country. 'Most men thought you were soliciting and sheered off,' she remembered, although as time went on they were mobbed by people desperate to appear on the box.

The two also forged intrepidly through strike mobs, covered disasters, met all sorts of VIPs, attended first nights (Lynne's speciality was show business) and brought real people as well as the famous into the nation's living rooms. She called stories of this sort, which mainly fell to her lot, 'Mother-of-10-in-a-council-house'.

When on camera Lynne favoured the bright, boldly patterned Horrockses dresses of the 1950s, with their drawstring necks and full skirts splayed out by stiffened petticoats, or neat, unshowy two-pieces with similarly capacious bottom halves – making it easier to clamber in and out of camera trucks. She was expected to shell out her own money for regular visits to the Knightsbridge salon of Mr Teasy-Weasy for a bubble-cut, blonde tips and streaks to look glamorous on camera. Still naïve for her age, Lynne as a reporter was given to terrible blunders, such as when she innocently asked the wife of the Swedish ambassador if her husband had big balls. '*Give,* dear! Or *throw*!' shouted her delighted male colleagues at her for the next week.

Interviewing Agatha Christie

The job was prestigious and exciting and both young women became minor celebrities, with Lynne once being sent up by comedian Benny Hill in a TV sketch featuring eager-beaver girl reporter 'Linseed Cranks'. But, unsurprisingly, neither Lynne nor Barbara received equal treatment with the men. They were paid less, patronised by the male team members, and given the softer issues to work on. Knowing that harder reporting was the way to further their careers, they had to push to cover the tougher stories such as industrial unrest or disasters. However, they were conscious at the same time that as women they were lucky to have the job in the first place. They were also flying in the face of convention by leaving home and living on their own – even having affairs, although doing so very doubtfully and, as Lynne commented, 'riven with guilt and fear' about the possible consequences in that pre-pill era. They were trying to be their own women, said Lynne in later years, to bring about change and make things happen:

...I remember it as a very exciting time – a pioneering, rule-breaking time, especially for the young. We 'girls' – young women – flew the nest early, created our own lifestyles and set our own moral compasses, built serious careers, travelled and, in general, refused to go back to the pre-war norm of being good little wives and mothers.

§

Eventually Lynne was given the boot from her on-screen role, reportedly for one faux pas too many, and from 1958 was put to work as a backroom journalist writing 'nasty ephemeral little scripts' for news items. Here, during a slow patch, she one day sat down at the special typewriter used to produce text for the teleprompter and, to see what the larger type looked like on the page, idly typed what became the first few words of *The L-Shaped Room*. One sentence led to another, and then another.

Half way down the page I discovered this girl is going to have a baby, and then I was off. But I had no plan, no design, it was simply something that grew.

I didn't know I had a book, I knew I had a situation, and quite an intriguing one...I only knew that this girl had found herself exiled from her own home. How this had happened, who her parents were, all this remained veiled for me until I actually came to them in the book.

The story she wrote is set in late 1950s London. Failed actress Jane Graham is pregnant after a loveless affair, and has been turned out of her comfortable middle-class home by her outraged father as 'no better than a street-woman'.

The L-shaped room she takes at the top of a dingy boarding house holds a washbasin which she also uses as a sink, a cigarette-scarred table, a chest of drawers missing a leg, a lumpy armchair and a tiny gas fire. The bed, Jane discovers, is infested. Her deliberate choice of an appalling place to live is a manifestation of her guilt, an acknowledgement that her unmarried pregnancy has put her beyond the pale. She has assumed society's punitive, negative attitude towards the unmarried mother:

I'd instinctively chosen an ugly, degraded district in which to find myself a room. There was the practical aspect of cheapness...But there was something more to it than that. In some obscure way I wanted to punish myself, I wanted to put myself in the setting that seemed proper to my situation.

The L-Shaped Room, Lynne Reid Banks, 1960

Jane nevertheless makes the room habitable and even attractive; it becomes her substitute for a family to love her. This is the theme and focus of the whole novel, Lynne was to explain: the transformation of the room is part of the transformation that Jane makes towards independence. She gradually meets the other inmates of the house, some of them outcasts from respectable society like her: the nasty landlady, black guitarist John in the next room, would-be novelist and troubled 'Angry Young Man' Toby downstairs, the prostitutes in the basement. Toby and John begin to play a part in her life, which Jane welcomes, although pretending the opposite – she needs them and they are important to her, despite her growing autonomy. After thinking she is having a miscarriage from gorging on curry, she decides once and for all to keep the baby. As she tries to hold down her PR job while coping with the difficult early months of her pregnancy she falls in love with Jewish writer Toby, beginning a complicated affair with him – and experiencing sexual pleasure for the first time – which is torn apart by his discovery of her pregnancy. The novel ends with the birth of the child, the situation with Toby unresolved but Jane now more independent and fully reconciled with her father. Her supportive Aunt Addy has died and left Jane her cottage; it is clear that she has the means and the skills to support herself and her child. The future looks positive.

§

Lynne was getting towards her late twenties when she began the novel and had started to think she might be on her own forever. She was learning to live with loneliness, she recalled in later life – not social loneliness, but the loneliness of being without a partner. She had entertained thoughts about having a child, or what it would be like to have a child, but one thing is clear: Lynne herself never became pregnant as a single young woman. The work is not autobiographical.

Lynne's main influence in life was her theoretically liberated ex-actress mother Pat, to whom she was very close and whom she always aimed to please; *The L-Shaped Room* is dedicated to her (and in memory of her father). Before the book came out Lynne gave Pat the manuscript to read. Her mother, of course, knew that Lynne had never given birth. After reading the manuscript she asked if Lynne intended to publish it under her own name, warning that people would think it was a thinly veiled piece of autobiography. Lynne replied scornfully that it was fiction: if she had written a book about a psychopathic murderer, she argued, would everyone think there were bodies under the floor? 'But it's very, very real,' said her mother, and was proved right. Reporters asked her where her baby was and for many years afterwards even people Lynne knew quite well wrote to ask, in various covert ways, whether there had actually been a pregnancy.

Other elements in the book were rooted in reality. Prior to the writing of the novel, when in her early twenties, Lynne had run away from home after a terrible quarrel with her mother and had spent the night in a boarding house in then down-at-heel Fulham. Walking through the rainy streets, in a highly emotional state and wanting to punish either herself or her family, she decided that she was going to move out and live in the most sordid, horrible place she could possibly find. Morning brought her back to her senses and she returned home, but the memory of Fulham remained and became her choice of location for the house in *The L-Shaped Room*.

The room itself was also based on an actual L-shaped room that Lynne had come across when searching for a flat for a friend. At the very top of a house she was looking at, which got worse and worse the higher the floor, were two rooms made from a single square: an inner one with no external window and an L-shaped one that was cramped and squalid. One quick look around the bend of the room was enough to decide Lynne against it and she fled, but the room imprinted itself on her memory. There had been something romantic about it, despite the squalor and the fact that she would not have contemplated living in such a place herself, used as she was to living somewhere 'quite grand, in its own way'. It triggered something, Lynne later commented: she wanted to know what existence would have been like in that sort of completely unfamiliar environment.

As for the characters, most were invented. Her heroine Jane has no mother in the book because Lynne wanted to avoid any kind of echo of her own mother, who had extracted a promise from her playwright daughter never to be written about. The father in the book is 'totally and completely' *not* her own father, Lynne emphasised. As for the black jazz guitarist John in the inner room next to Jane's in the boarding house, Lynne claimed that at the time of writing she had not even met anyone black. Jane's Aunt Addy in the book, on the other hand, was based to some extent on Lynne's much loved Great Aunt Adelaide and was therefore an exception to the list of invented characters. For Lynne, Addy was a very real and very loving character who probably deserved a book to herself.

The novel is well written, in a straightforward, almost reporter-like style which at the same time is funny, sad, and utterly gripping, as though it is all happening there and then to the reader. The L-shaped room is real, the characters are real, and Jane's dilemma is real. It is a classic work about courage, self-discovery, and ultimately love, both between Toby and Jane, and between the three friends – and between Jane and her estranged father, who poignantly learn to care for each other for the first time in their lives.

But it is also very much of its era, with the attitudes shown towards abortion and pregnancy outside of marriage perhaps key to the novel's continuing fascination. The condescending private doctor whom Jane consults to confirm her suspected pregnancy assumes that she must want a termination, and casually arranges for her to see another doctor who will countersign a certificate attesting that she is psychologically or physically unfit to have a child (the only route to legal abortion in mainland Britain at the time). The termination would then follow at a private clinic – for a huge sum of money, of course, which the doctor points out would be the same if she went to a 'back-street merchant in Paddington'. Jane lets rip at him, furious that the doctor has not even examined her, let alone asked her if she actually wants to get rid of the baby. After some argument back and forth the doctor – not all bad – gives Jane some advice and the address of the Society for Unmarried Mothers and sends her on her way, gaining the moral high ground by refusing to take any payment. Once embarked on her road to becoming an unmarried mother Jane must then struggle with the judgement she meets as regards her lack of a wedding ring, and to start with finds it a hard task to be honest about her single status.

Lynne personally, of course, through Jane as her mouthpiece, makes absolutely no judgement about sex outside marriage and a woman on her own deciding to have a child. Quite the reverse: the way the novel is written cannot help but elicit sympathy for the single, pregnant heroine battling to keep her baby in the face of prejudice. In this Lynne was far ahead of her time, and equally so in allowing Jane to feel sexual desire and enjoy an erotic and tender relationship with Toby. However, she was not far ahead of her time as regards racism and homophobia – apart from her dislike throughout the novel of anti-Semitism (the most unattractive character in the book, Jane's former lover, taunts Toby by calling him 'Jew-boy', and Jane explodes with fury when Toby suggests she might not want to marry him because he is Jewish). With this one exception, the author in other respects showed herself all too subject to the prejudices of the era: Jane worries that if her baby is a boy he may grow up homosexual through lack of a father, while black musician John is depicted as almost a simpleton. Jane refers to John's 'powerful negro smell' and his wide grin (she even wonders if black men have more teeth), while Toby compares him to a child and a monkey. These are aspects of the novel that considerably jar on the modern reader.

But at the same time Jane rebukes herself for reacting with terror on first catching a glimpse of John through the little high window which separates their rooms – 'After all, why in God's name should a black face be more alarming than a white one?' – and as the novel progresses John is gradually revealed to be no different from anyone else and a man who is kind, sensitive and loyal. When Jane eventually realises he is homosexual she is surprised to feel no 'revulsion' and in fact believes that it is this very aspect that makes him such a true friend. Racial prejudice and homophobia are certainly there in the novel, as they almost universally were in works of the period, but through her compassionate characterisation Lynne's true humanity and tolerance win through.

§

It took Lynne nearly two years to write, not in her comfortable flat in Kensington but in the office, rattling away late at night with her typewriter on her knees after the last bulletin at ITN. She discovered that the usual truism of escaping from real-life troubles through reading or writing did not work for her: rather, she used her fiction as a *worse* situation to escape to. Her troubles were not nearly as bad as her heroine's, she saw, and when she returned from Jane's her own paled in comparison.

As the novel neared completion Lynne became very fed up with the whole project, thinking it 'lousy'. Although an infrequent drinker, by the time she reached the last chapter she was swigging from an old bottle of Slivovitz brandy just to get through it. It was a case of forcing herself to the finish, putting aside her own concerns and concentrating on her fictional heroine. She needed to describe several months of Jane's pregnancy but at a certain point felt that she had run the whole L-shaped room setting to a dead end; another location was needed to broaden out the narrative, so she gave Jane a stay in the country with her Aunt Addy. Once the book was at last done she was left with no real hopes of it, but sent the manuscript off – in a very messy state – to the agent she had retained from her play-writing days. It was accepted by publishers Chatto & Windus, described by Lynne as one of the greatest thrills of her life, and published in 1960.

With her total lack of expectation Lynne was stunned by the novel's generally glowing reception. The *Tatler* aligned her with Shelagh Delaney, dubbing the novel 'a sort of middling-rich-woman's *Taste of Honey*' (the lack of any class war in fact losing it points from the left) and for the *New Statesman* the book was 'touching and competent...ambitious and mature', although remarking that Jane can move on from the shabby bedsit but not so the other characters, so steeped in poverty that they have little hope of a similarly happy ending. Across the Atlantic the *New York Times* was impressed by the work's 'bright, warm prose'. The *Times Literary Supplement* did accuse Lynne of magazine-story improbabilities and of substituting clichés for crucial reality, and the *Sunday Times* questioned the wisdom of writing about 'broken-down people living in an awful broken-down house in Fulham', but the reading public rushed to pull it from the shelves and the novel continues to sell and win plaudits even to the present day. 'This is an angry tale in many ways, with an inextinguishable fire of authenticity,' enthusiastically commented *The Independent on Sunday* well into the twenty-first century: Lynne's 'journalistic style, as well as her eye for detail, is perfectly suited to the theme, and a documentary feel rather than a poetic register strengthens the impact of her message'.

Lynne very quickly sold the film rights, to the utter astonishment of her male colleagues in the ITN newsroom, whom she recalled standing frozen in surprise when she told them. (One of these was the young broadcaster Ludovic Kennedy, who used to lean over Lynne's chair when she was writing the novel and read out the juicy bits for the general entertainment.)

Bryan Forbes was the director, and he also wrote the screenplay – changing so much from the novel that Lynne was aghast:

It was so entirely different...when I first saw it, I was utterly shattered.

The plot stayed much the same but the setting was moved to Notting Hill. Jane was turned into a Frenchwoman – in order to give the role to sultry Leslie Caron – while Toby morphed into a Yorkshireman, played by lean and brooding young hellraiser Tom Bell. Jane's father and Aunt Addy were wiped out altogether. Another resident of the house in the novel, retired opera company wardrobe mistress Mavis, became instead a lesbian ex-actress belting out the First World War song *Take Me Back to Dear Old Blighty,* as a former crop-haired landlady of Bryan's had once done, resplendent in Tommy uniform, when he was in digs as a young actor. These new conceptions of Bryan Forbes' were not less interesting characters in themselves, Lynne acknowledged, and were possibly even more interesting than the originals – Bryan laid it on with a thicker trowel, in her opinion – but she had lived with them for a long time while writing the book and had a great affection for them; they had become extremely real to her, which made the changes very upsetting.

But what really shocked Lynne was the total loss of Jane's growing independence, the meaning and focus of her novel. At the end of the screenplay Jane decides to return with the baby to her conventional Catholic family in France, who she suspects will try to pass her off as a tragic widow. Lynne insisted Jane would never have done this. 'I found it a travesty of my book and it took me twenty years to forgive Bryan for that,' she said. She did, in the end, and was generous enough to praise his *L-Shaped Room* as a good film that stood the test of time.

Leslie Caron was of the same mind about the character she was playing, feeling that Jane as portrayed in Bryan's script was too passive and tame, and ought to rebel. She succeeded in convincing Bryan to change at least one scene to this effect. She enjoyed the drama of the role, finding that her own youthful experience in shabby rooms when on the road with a ballet company came flooding back to inform her performance. There were difficulties, however. Although it was 'a plum of a part', making the film was gritty and demanding and obliged her to work very long hours, so much so that it became difficult for Leslie to keep her emotional balance: she found it 'harrowing, very tiring'. After a dramatic scene she often needed to sleep, and would curl up in the middle of the set with the electricians and other technicians calling out to each other, as comforting to Leslie as a lullaby.

She told the film's producer, Richard Attenborough (brother of David), that she would always be unable to work on the first day of her period, which of course did not go down too well. He asked her to supply a list of dates so that shooting could be arranged around them, which she did, but one evening had to phone him to say that a date was wrong and she would not be on set the following morning. Richard refused to cancel Leslie's normal car, cannily telling her that it would arrive at its usual time and adding 'Whether you choose to come is, of course, entirely up to you, darling.' She complied, turning up with puffy face and dark circles under her eyes and described by another member of the production team as looking grumpy and 'very French'. It was clear that any close-ups were out of the question and she was sent home. For the remainder of the filming she and Richard hardly spoke.

Exterior work could also be challenging. 'Filming in Notting Hill in those days, it was a total slum,' Leslie remembered. 'Every building was cruddy and peeling, with great big chunks of plaster falling off...those old Victorian and Edwardian terraced houses, I thought it was the East End we were filming in.' Notting Hill was still recovering from the recent race riots, a period of conflict between Teddy Boys brandishing bicycle chains and Caribbean immigrants armed with knives. The shivering newcomers had moved into crowded terraced houses and been subject to exploitation by unscrupulous slum landlords; racial tension followed, coming to a head in the Notting Hill riot of 1958 when night after night mobs of white locals carried out attacks on immigrant homes. A number understandably fought back, and were among those arrested for grievous bodily harm and possession of offensive weapons. (Early in 1959, in an attempt to ease tension, local volunteers organised a 'Caribbean Carnival' – precursor to the later Notting Hill Carnival.)

Leslie suspected, wrongly, that the story in *The L-Shaped Room* was Lynne's own experience, and also that a Frenchwoman had been chosen to play the unmarried mother – casting which angered the press, when there were perfectly good English actresses to choose from – in order to make what Leslie saw as an 'extremely shocking' plotline more acceptable to the public. The film was certainly very frank about the pregnancy. When the American columnist Sheilah Graham visited the set she gave an audible gasp on seeing Leslie's padded nine-month stomach: no American star had ever shown herself on screen so bulky with baby, whatever the role may have demanded. It was courageous of Leslie, who for extra authenticity insisted on wearing on set an old blue nylon dressing gown that she had worn when pregnant herself, one that remained visibly distended from the bump. Leslie also gave a short but realistic portrayal of the agony of giving birth, again very unusual at the time. Male actors in westerns and other action films had licence to express pain with crude honesty, she pointed out, but a discreet euphemism was all Hollywood good taste would allow to women. Leslie wanted to break the rules.

The script had to be submitted for censorship, and Bryan chose to consult the British Board of Film Censors in the pre-production stage. The screenplay was a fine piece of writing, wrote the Board in their reply in April 1962, but the film could only be considered in the explicit 'X' category. Four closely typed pages of detailed changes were required to get the film passed: the removal of religious expletives, for example, the substitution of 'tart' for 'whore' and the removal of the twice-repeated word 'sod' (although not 'arse', which the Board helpfully explained was permissible in X films).

As might be expected in that era, the issues of contraception, abortion and pregnancy came in for special attention. As an exception a discussion of contraceptives was permitted because the exchange occurs between Jane and her doctor (although in the end the scene did not appear in the final film). The Board was equally anxious as a rule to avoid any references to possible means of abortion, but did allow the scene in which Jane takes an abortifacient pill because the nature of the pill is not spelt out and in any case does not work. As for the pregnancy, it was requested that sex scenes between Jane and Toby be handled with extra care as the audience would know that Jane was expecting: nudity and semi-nudity should be avoided. The way in which Toby and their friend John touch Jane in her pregnant condition would likewise need to be handled 'sensitively and movingly'.

It was also pointed out that as audiences often had a physical reaction to the sight and sound of people being sick, discretion in this matter was advisable. Jane was allowed to say 'I'm up to here with milk', but without any visual images which might make the line 'offensive', and Bryan was warned not to show her in an ungainly condition (he did). A late scene in the film in which a heavily pregnant Jane is examined by a doctor should contain as little detail as possible, as pregnancy was inclined to be 'somewhat degrading for a woman'.

As regards sexual references in general, the Board objected to the proposed line 'That's the sort of thing that makes me want to fornicate right in the middle of Westminster Abbey during a Royal Wedding.' Care must be taken with the visuals of people fondling each other, the office further advised: no breast-rubbing or thigh-rubbing, and no 'copulatory dancing'. The scene in which Mavis refers to the love of her life while indicating a photograph of a woman was deemed acceptable because Mavis is talking about love and not about sex, although it was suggested that the scene be shot in such a way as to make it possible for the photograph to be omitted should the Board later require it (and in the event the photograph does not get shown on camera, although the viewer is clearly meant to infer that Mavis' lover was female). Concern was also expressed about the scene showing John listening through the wall to sounds of Toby and Jane having sex, in effect warning against any hint that he might be enjoying it.

An examination of the letter shows that in nearly every case a robust 'Ignore' was scrawled in the margin at the side of these strictures, presumably by Bryan, but the finished film does demonstrate a somewhat softened approach from the original script and Leslie wore

Elastoplast over her nipples for a sex scene (possibly then routine in film-making). Many years later Bryan was to look back at the Board's edicts as 'messages from another planet'. The then head of the British Board of Film Censors was ultimately to agree. '*The L-Shaped Room* was frank in its dialogue about sex,' he wrote in his 1973 memoir, 'and there was a sex scene which had implications of nudity which in retrospect was very mild.'

The film, in atmospheric monochrome and accompanied by a swelling Brahms concerto, came out later in 1962. Despite the changes it was viewed as very frank – 'Sex is not a forbidden word!' promised the posters – especially in America, where many movie houses simply refused to run it. The *Australian Women's Weekly* liked the sad, indeterminate ending, which gave the film the realism 'one has come to expect from first-class-British films' (although declaring that anyone who had ever roomed in London on the cheap would sympathise with Leslie Caron and the odd bunch of boarders she had to live with).

At home it was enthusiastically received, for the most part. The *Illustrated London News* saw the film as investing bedsit squalor with its own kind of poetry and of course detected similarities to the film version of *A Taste of Honey*, as did the British Film Institute in its *Sight and Sound* review. However, the BFI deemed the film to have little to say about contemporary life in a London bedsitter. Bryan Forbes' rather capricious direction disappointingly spilled over into melodrama, observed their critic: bugs in the bed, bangings on the wall, John's black face looking through the high-up little window between his and Jane's attic rooms (all of which were actually in the original book and not inventions of Bryan). Neither direction nor script was ever tough enough to succeed in suggesting loneliness, the review continued, and Bryan Forbes' obvious talent for drawing likeable performances from his actors tended to work against him, in that the people in the house were all cinematic 'characters' – Cicely Courtneidge's self-contained old trouper Mavis, Emlyn Williams' unprincipled gynaecologist, Patricia Phoenix's gregarious blonde prostitute.

However, Leslie Caron was appealing as the idealistic girl who wins the battle to produce her baby against often unbelievable odds, the BFI judged, and Tom Bell exactly pinpointed the frustrated attitudes of a broke, would-be intellectual who cannot afford a bottle of cheap wine, let alone a potential wife with child. When the film was soberly engaged in telling a simple, romantic story, the review concluded, it did achieve a certain assurance as well as considerable charm, and viewers would like the film for its inherent wholesomeness. The film was not all gloom and shadow, agreed the *Times Literary Supplement*. The good-natured, indulgent tolerance of the poor to one another was admirably conveyed, and, while the comedy might be conventional, the lines were consistently sharp and entertaining.

For the *Tatler*, though, Leslie Caron was the wrong choice to play Jane, her 'general air of fastidiousness' making it unlikely that she would ever have tolerated the bug-ridden squalor of the bedsit. Leslie nevertheless won a Golden Globe award for Best Actress and a BAFTA in the same category. BAFTA night at the London Hilton was unfortunately marred by an inebriated Tom Bell heckling Prince Philip, presiding over the award-giving. Tom, seated at a table with Leslie, Bryan and Richard Attenborough, called out something like 'Give us a joke, Philip!' as the prince was giving a speech, repeating it when ignored. Prince Philip replied, with good humour, to the effect that if they wanted jokes they should have hired a comedian. The audience erupted in applause. Leslie later apologised to the Prince on her co-star's behalf – 'Tom was a little merry,' she explained – but in the opinion of contemporary commentators, Tom's actions had scuppered his chance of a successful career (not so, in the event).

Not long after the film came out Leslie herself plunged into a tempestuous affair with actor Warren Beatty, which led to the break-up of her marriage. She went on to an ever more successful career as an actress and also proved to be a talented writer. Brock Peters, playing John, was to become most famous for his role as the man falsely accused of raping a white woman in *To Kill a Mockingbird*.

The L-Shaped Room remains a moving and very watchable film, ending, as did the novel, with Jane going back to the room to collect her things and meeting the new tenant, a hard-faced girl played by Bryan's wife Nanette Newman. Other changes from the novel include Jane deciding to take a pill in an attempt to abort, which she rejected doing in Lynne's original work, and for some reason giving birth to a girl instead of a boy (with some interesting historical touches for twenty-first-century viewers: the doctor who delivers Jane's baby walks into the labour room with a fag in his hand and after the birth Jane gets to stay a whole week in hospital). Another intriguing departure from the novel is that jazz guitarist John's homosexuality is only hinted at. Although not remarked on at the time, reviewers in the decades to come would point out that Bryan Forbes' film actually eliminated what is generally seen as the racism and homophobia of the novel.

Culturally, *The L-Shaped Room*, both film and novel, remains lodged in the national consciousness sometimes not so much for the story itself but for its archetypal account of living in dismal digs cheek by jowl with strangers on the other side of flimsy partitioning. After the two world wars housing shortage was a critical issue for Britain, leading to the proliferation of often sub-standard living spaces created by dividing up larger areas. In traditional boarding or lodging houses residents ate together, had their cleaning and laundry seen to by the landlady and sometimes socialised with each other by playing cards or listening to the radio in a communal area; the newer concept of 'bedsitter' was, as the name suggests, more self-contained: a combination bedroom, living room and kitchen, usually equipped with cast-off rickety furniture, probably flea-ridden. Often tenanted by the young, bedsitters were cheaper and more independent, but also grimmer and lonelier. Certain areas of London came to be known as 'bedsitter land': Notting Hill, Pimlico, Islington. In 1961 *Cooking in a Bedsitter* came out from young journalist Katharine Whitehorn and was an instant classic with its tips for dealing with lingering smells, fetching water from a shared bathroom and storing foods that go off quickly. Lynne Reid Banks' vivid description in the novel of living and cooking in shabby digs, surrounded by strangers whose every move is audible – a way of life endured by Lynne during her years on the road as a touring actress – somehow nailed the experience for all time. Lynne's L-shaped room was as much a character as any of the inhabitants, wrote an academic: the premier example of the starring role played by partitioning in a 'world of shadowy staircases, public telephones in the hallway, landlords' notices in windows, and, crucially, walls that are always too thin'. For Paul McCartney, reading about Lynn's characters recalled the Beatles' own experience of this kind of existence during their early years of touring: 'You could read *The L-Shaped Room* and totally associate,' he said. 'This is what I'm doing! This is totally about me! It's true. It was an exact parallel; young professionals in a rooming house.'

The *L-Shaped Room* film was to be yet another influence for singer Morrissey: in 1986, Cicely Courtneidge's rendition in the film of *Take Me Back to Dear Old Blighty* was appropriated by the Smiths for a soundbite opener to their *The Queen is Dead* album. Sixties films like *A Taste of Honey* and *The L-Shaped Room*, about Northern, working-class people, were a sign to Morrissey that there was room for someone from his background and with his accent: before these films, actors all had a very clipped, theatre-school way of talking, he commented. In 1985, when he was concentrating on journalism rather than music, Morrissey interviewed Patricia Phoenix about her prostitute role in *The L-Shaped Room* for a magazine article. Pat had been playing Elsie Tanner in Granada Television's *Coronation Street* at the time and she told Morrissey that a stipulation in her contract did not allow her to accept other roles without permission, so when Bryan Forbes offered her such a tempting part she sneaked off and did it in four days without telling anyone.

Of Pat's portrayal of Elsie Tanner, Morrissey wrote:

Elsie was the screen's first 'angry young woman'; a wised-up, tongue-lashing cylindrical tempest, sewn into cheap and overstuffed dresses, harnessed by severe poverty, staunchly defending her fatherless children, devouring a blizzard of temporary husbands in dour Salford council dwellings.

§

The troubles that Lynne was experiencing when writing *The L-Shaped Room* may have concerned her deepening relationship with a young Anglo-Jewish sculptor, Chaim Stephenson, whom she met in 1960 during a year he spent studying in Britain (according to Lynne, well after she had already created the character of Toby the Jewish writer in the novel). Her mother Pat disliked Chaim, in her daughter's opinion because he was Jewish and working-class, and because as a struggling young artist he was unlikely to be able to maintain Lynne in appropriate middle-class style. Lynne still reproached herself for missing the war and remaining in ignorance about the Holocaust; she remained intrigued by Israel and had already travelled there with the £100 she received as an advance for *The L-Shaped Room*. Her love for Chaim cemented this fascination and she decided to emigrate to be with him on his kibbutz (or 'chased after him', in her own words). Pat was horrified. Lynne was back living at home and would listen to her mother in the next bedroom, sobbing her eyes out night after night as her daughter's departure drew nearer. She was about to lose her only child to an unknown future, but it was not only that: passionately patriotic and a lifelong Conservative, Pat viewed kibbutz life as a form of communism, and also believed that by leaving Britain her daughter would be wasting her writing talent and never be able to produce anything significant about her own country.

Resolute, Lynne left for Israel in 1962, leaving behind an agent and publisher equally disgruntled about her disappearance into the wilderness. She was not immune from regret herself. She loved the success she was having, which was very difficult to leave:

My first book, The L-Shaped Room, had been made into a successful film, I had had plays on TV and radio, and my second novel was getting good notices. And off I'd gone to Israel – non-Jew though I was – to live the simple life with Chaim Stephenson, my Jewish lover...

She began her life on the kibbutz, or collective community, in Western Galilee as a worker in the chicken houses, too tired at night to do anything but fall into bed after eating in the communal dining hall. She was eventually assigned to teaching English to schoolchildren. She and Chaim were married in 1965 and produced three sons, handing over at least the first of them to a 'baby house' for communal rearing (a system Lynne continually rebelled against). Living in the Middle East she also had to endure cross border raids, occasional shelling and Chaim leaving to fight in the Six-Day Arab-Israeli War of 1967. Despite all this, Lynne was to say that she was happier in her nine years in Israel than she had ever been before or ever would be in the future – though admitting that her original intention had been to lure Chaim away from the kibbutz because she couldn't quite see herself doing dirty farm work out in the country. In the end she came to feel that the existence was the right one for her:

Living in a kibbutz, working the land, teaching and having my babies in that 'alien' country that I came to love so much, was a sublimation for my lingering feelings of guilt for having missed the War...

The family returned to Britain in the early 1970s, intending to remain for just one year. The boys were completely disoriented in England and because of her former communal way of living on the kibbutz, Lynne herself had never run her own home or looked after her own family. It was a difficult time, with Lynne having to return to some serious writing to help with finances, but eventually things settled and it became clear they would not go back to Israel. Relations had been mended with her mother, although Lynne always felt that she disliked having Jewish grandchildren. Anti-semitism was a disease, Lynne observed, a virus that could infect an otherwise healthy psyche and a curse that could mar healthy, happy relationships.

Ultimately Lynne was to be mainly a children's writer, her most famous work, *The Indian in the Cupboard*, becoming a very successful film in 1995. Writing for children was easier and much more fun, she discovered. She did still write for older audiences, including a 1977 episode for the TV series *Seven Faces of Woman* – following in the footsteps of fellow contributor to the series Shelagh Delaney in 1974.

§

On a similar theme to her first and most famous novel Lynne was to write *The Unborn*, a play exploring whether abortion can ever be justified, and also two more books about Jane – in order, she said, to see how a woman in that situation manages. In *The Backward Shadow* Jane is living with baby David in Aunt Addy's old cottage, still trying to resolve her relationship with Toby and struggling to make a go of a new business with a friend; in *Two Is Lonely* David is eight and Jane is contemplating marriage. Jazz guitarist Johnny makes a further appearance in both novels as a now greatly valued friend – the customary racism of the era now more muted. Both sequels are witty and well written, frank about female sexuality, and worth chasing down for readers interested in Jane's subsequent life and loves.

The answer to how Jane managed as a single parent was not too well, Lynne discovered as she wrote the books, and in later life she was forthright in declaring her opinion that a child should have both mother and father: it was better to wait until there was a partner and a set-up to bring a baby into, she believed. Once a mother herself, she could look back and see *The L-Shaped Room* as the rose-tinted view of single parenthood it really was. At the time, having a baby as a single woman had appeared to her as rather glamorous: an independent, even heroic act. Jane *chooses* to have the baby, rather than abort or have it adopted, and when Lynne wrote the book before having her own children she thought it was the right decision. She changed her mind. 'Any woman who does it voluntarily must be mad,' she said in her fifties, although admiring women to whom it happened involuntarily and who managed to cope. She had found it very hard bringing up her own three sons, even with help. In fact looking back, Lynne wondered that her character had rejected abortion so readily:

...neither Jane nor I knew what we were doing. If I had known what bringing up children...was actually like, I doubt if I could have ended the book so glibly, nor dismissed the abortionist so indignantly...

Not that many women were natural mothers, she believed. Given her time again, she would not choose to be a mother because of the terrible emotional responsibility.

When Lynne re-read her book in much later life she thought it 'pleasing', but as though reading a book written by another person and about a completely different era. 'It might as well have been a hundred years ago as fifty,' she observed. There were elements in the book that she found quite startling, such as the way she had written the black character Johnny. She had made him rather too primitive in his speech and in other ways, Lynne realised, and although she was very fond of him, and thought his character one of the best in the film because the closest to her original conception, there was definitely something almost racist in her treatment. She would never dream of writing like that now:

One of the reasons is that PC [political correctness] *has intervened. Thank God it has. PC is nothing more or less than making you examine your bigotries and not hurt people's feelings.*

She could only explain what she termed her 'shocking' portrayal of John by saying that in those days other races were regarded not as inherently inferior but as just deeply different. It was like viewing people across a great gulf, said Lynne in retrospect, more so even than across the class divide. At that time there was no abhorrence of racial prejudice, it existed and it came out in her book. Now she found it shameful and embarrassing. However, prejudice was of the era and her characters would have reacted in the manner she depicted, Lynne maintained. It was very much a period piece. The author should not be blamed for what characters do, say and feel.

§

Lynne always rejected the 'Angry Young Woman' label and distanced herself from John Osborne, at least (hardly surprising, considering the bad blood between them). While she knew John 'and all that crowd' quite well when young, and had envied them having their books published, their actual writing and lifestyle had not influenced her. It was all very different from her own take on life, she observed.

Far from being angry, the mature Lynne in fact regretted her lack of feminism when writing *The L-Shaped Room*. 'I should have gone to the barricades and fought for feminism...I would like to have felt that I worked towards women's rights, but I didn't.' She frankly admitted that for a long time she believed men were the superior sex ('what a joke!'), only later coming to think the exact opposite and that men were probably the most dangerous creatures on the planet. But while not exactly manning the barricades Lynne nevertheless felt that she had written a feminist book unconsciously, and was proud of having done so. 'We really were pioneers,' she observed. As an independent young news reporter she was actually living the life that feminists were theorising about, she pointed out, trying to be her own woman, and believed that deep in her gut she had known that change must come.

But she regretted her absence from Britain for the best of the 1960s.

I would have enjoyed the swinging Sixties and got rid of all the guilt trips that we had about sex in the 1950s...I think it's rather sad in a way that I was away for it.

The Pumpkin Eater

Penelope Mortimer

'You don't care about me, all you care about is the bills being paid and that great fucking army of children that I'm supposed to support and work my guts out for, so I can't even take a bath in peace, I can't eat a bloody meal without them whining and slobbering all over the table, I can't even go to bed with you without one of them comes barging in in the middle.'

The Pumpkin Eater, Penelope Mortimer, 1962

§

Penelope Mortimer was most definitely angry when she wrote *The Pumpkin Eater*.

She was the daughter of highly eccentric parents, each from a family of eleven children – one of the few things they had in common, according to Penelope. Arthur Fletcher was a clergyman who did not believe in God, five years younger than his wife Amy who in 1918 gave birth to her second child Penelope at the age of forty-two. In preparation for the birth she sent her first child Paul, then only four years old, away to boarding school, never again to live at home. As her father was sent from parish to parish Penelope spent her early girlhood in various vicarages around the country; in one of these her mother started a residential nursery called 'The Little People's Garden' for the children of soldiers and civil servants serving the British Empire overseas. Penelope – known as Pegs – felt no jealousy, joining in with the children's games and story times and finding it all 'very enjoyable'.

Her parents' marriage was unhappy; Penelope had no memory of them ever sharing a bedroom, and could only remember one occasion when her mother did not move away from her father's touch (Amy was later to fall in love with a woman). Between the ages of eight and about seventeen she was molested by her father, in her own words because his deprivation had become 'unbearable':

It seldom went further than sloppy kisses and inexpert groping in my school knickers, but I hated it and for the next fifty years was under the sad misapprehension that I hated him.

In fact, she realised later, her father's shame and humiliation affected her far worse than the actual abuse. They were years of 'difficulty and discomfort', as she described them in her autobiography. Her mother's abhorrence of sex made it impossible for Penelope to tell her what was going on. In her maturity Penelope was surprisingly forgiving towards Arthur, who she believed suffered from the situation more than she did.

After a series of boarding schools, some better than others, beautiful seventeen-year-old Penelope was signed up for secretarial training in London, where she initially lived a lonely life in a girls' hostel. But by now seriously interested in being a writer, she persuaded her parents to allow her to switch to a journalism course at University College. Sharing a flat with her brother, Penelope slowly recovered from a first love affair and went on to enjoy several more, frequently getting engaged 'for as long as a week, sometimes to two people at once'. The journalism course was abandoned and she found work as a secretary, but, looking for stability, at the age of nineteen she married Reuters reporter Charles Dimont. She dressed entirely in black for the ceremony, a 'foolish little gesture of self-assertion'. The night before the wedding, sharing a hotel room with her mother, Penelope noticed that Amy was looking at her with an expression of 'infinite pity':

'To think,' she said, 'that tomorrow night you will be <u>sharing a bed</u>!' She chose to overlook the fact that I had been living with Charles for some months – it was marriage that appalled her, the prospect of lifelong intimacy.

In 1938 Penelope gave birth to a baby girl, and when World War II kicked off a year later she returned to live with her parents while conscientious objector Charles worked in London. At home Penelope's mother virtually took over the mothering role, despite what Penelope called Amy's lack of 'every maternal quality' except the provision of regular meals – although as a grandmother she proved more demonstrative. Penelope was left with nothing to do but scribble, producing her first attempt at a novel in 1939. It was rejected, with what she termed the usual encouraging 'sops' that she showed promise and distinction. She immediately began on another.

A second daughter was born, the family of four by this time on a more independent footing. Then Charles introduced his young wife to a friend working on chemical warfare at Porton Down, Kenneth Harrison, who was immediately struck with attractive, dark-haired Penelope. To Kenneth she was

...witty, refreshing, elegant and...anyhow I fell in love with her, seriously, practically at first meeting. She...began to favour me and no more needs to be said.

Her third daughter, 'a pint-sized Harrison', was born as the war was nearing its end, husband Charles assuming the baby was his. Contraception during the discreet affair with Kenneth had failed: it was long before the pill or the coil, Penelope thought condoms awkward and ridiculous and she disliked inserting her Dutch cap just as sex was getting interesting. 'The only method left, apart from *coitus interruptus*, mathematics [meaning the calculation of fertile periods in order to avoid them] and chastity, was a dissolving pessary which could be shoved in with the minimum foresight and fuss.' The baby was christened a Dimont.

Two years later came her first published novel, *Johanna*, under the name Penelope Dimont. It 'died at birth', said Penelope. When she confessed her third child's true parentage to Charles the marriage, never very successful, began to founder, and she started a passionate relationship with the married poet Randall Swingler. During this, sitting one day in the garden of her country cottage painting a coal scuttle, Penelope looked up to see a horse looming over the hedge. Seated on the horse was a young man in glasses who introduced himself as John Mortimer, a friend of Randall's. She told him she had run out of bread and he offered to fetch her some.

Penelope was then twenty-nine, John twenty-four, a promising writer studying to be a barrister – in her description a 'clever, skinny, excitable youth'. What seemed ordinary life to Penelope – marriage, children, love affairs, writing – seemed exotic to the public school- and Oxford-educated only child of a barrister. He, too, fell in love with Penelope but thanks to Randall another baby was again on its way. A man only had to hang his trousers over the end of the bed for her to get pregnant, she would remark. On being told of the baby Randall promptly disappeared, and John suggested getting rid of the child. Penelope loved babies and had an instinctive horror of abortion (although fervently supportive in principle), but she agreed to go and see a woman in Chelsea who according to John would do it for 'a reasonable fee'. Once there, she refused to go through with it and bolted. She and John were already lovers and began living together following the arrival of Penelope's fourth daughter – born prematurely, in Penelope's words possibly as a result of an over-active sex life.

They were married in 1949 on the day Penelope's divorce from Charles was finalised, and soon another baby was on the way, their first child together – another girl.

John was infatuated with his sophisticated older wife and greatly relished his tumultuous new family, making meals, taking the children for walks, reading them stories – he was 'remarkably tolerant', stated Penelope (at least at that stage). As the 1950s dawned, John and Penelope found themselves fully occupied with their family of five girls but also as time went on with their increasingly successful writing, the domestic front often a source of irritation for Penelope when she wanted to work, although she was to comment that at this point writing was not necessarily her priority. There were friends, parties and holidays abroad and both were happy, if sometimes at loggerheads (but ever eager to make it up in bed). 'We make love, we quarrel, we make it up, we quarrel, we make it up, we make love,' said Penelope.

Then John started to get restless. Becoming the father of such a large family had been a staggering change for the young bachelor, not least in terms of money. 'There were so many of them,' he remarked, 'that bills for things which I had never bought before – luxuries such as Vim, Ostermilk, plastic knickers and bicky-pegs – seemed huge.' He spent his twenties being a father and working hard to meet the new costs. Now, feeling anxious about wasted time and opportunities, he embarked on an affair with the divorced wife of jazz musician Humphrey Lyttelton. Penelope was devastated:

All my life I had been used to absolute power, exclusive attention. Who was I, if I wasn't unique? No one I could recognise. John was correct in saying I was like someone who had lost an empire. I fixed the pieces of my self-esteem together in some semblance of the original, but the image was never quite the same.

She described John as 'bewildered' by the grief and loss his affair caused her, and later observed that he did not take his affairs seriously himself and therefore did not expect her to. Reconciliation followed and a son was born in April 1955. Once again they were plunged into nappies and sleepless nights. They both began to take drugs – 'uppers' – to get through their days (and nights) and in early 1956 Penelope attempted suicide by taking an overdose, an event ascribed to severe postnatal depression. After a break abroad she returned to find that she had far less to occupy her: in addition to a new nanny, John had hired a cook and a charlady to provide more help in the house. She began to see a psychoanalyst, though not for long: her 'sense of the ridiculous....got in the way'.

The marriage continued, not always unhappily. There were spreads in glossy magazines on the brilliant Mortimers, the predictable label 'mother of six' permanently affixed to Penelope. Both were now well known as writers, John for his novels and plays and Penelope, over time, for her own increasingly successful novels, her book reviews in the *Sunday Times*, her column of parental advice for the *Evening Standard* (called Five Girls and a Boy), and her series of stories for *The New Yorker*. They had become an item for the press, an enviable, golden young couple about town: John the clever barrister and rising literary star, Penelope fecund, talented and beautiful – once mistaken for Audrey Hepburn – and their large and contented family.

§

Penelope's fiction for *The New Yorker* was mostly semi-autobiographical, as Penelope herself admitted:

None of the stories could accurately be described as fiction; the moment I fabricated or attempted to get away from direct experience The New Yorker regretfully turned it down.

There was no need to look for ideas, she was to explain in her memoirs. She mined her life for incidents 'with a beginning, a middle and an end, finding even the dreariest days contained nuggets of irony, farce, unpredictable behaviour'. *Such a Super Evening*, for example, one of Penelope's stories published during this period, was about a glitteringly famous couple invited to dinner by an unassuming housewife who can't believe her luck when they accept. The fictional Mathiesons are nothing short of 'an institution', they 'symbolize a whole way of life'. They are hugely successful writers in an array of different genres – novels, plays, film scripts, criticism – both of them full of energy, humour, and intelligence, and the parents of eight remarkable children (called, in a pastiche of middle-class naming, Sophia, Simon, Emma, Henrietta, Sebastian, Philippa, Piers and Adam). But as dinner progresses the glamorous Mathiesons expose themselves as they truly are, the husband revealing that his wife is dependent on pills for her celebrated energy and that not all of the children, who to avoid tax he has made shareholders in their limited company, are his – at which point the furiously smoking wife dissolves in bitter hysterics. Her husband, she has already let fly, gets up not at six as stated but at midday, just in time for lunch at the Caprice. The embarrassed guests begin to melt away but the Mathiesons carry on, 'two clever robots packed with enough talk for a week'.

In another story, *Saturday Lunch with the Brownings*, wife and mother Madge Browning tries to conciliate her husband William as he becomes ever more irritated by a house heaving with distracting and annoying children. She it is who has to arrange the plan for each day, the entertainment, meals, expeditions, and safety from disturbance. As well as this unequal distribution of household tasks, William spoils his own darling daughter

Bessie and calls Madge's biological daughters 'delinquent little bitches'. The *Sunday Times* review of the collection in which the story appeared, likewise entitled *Saturday Lunch with the Brownings*, found the married couples in her tales 'trivially embittered' and asked why they didn't just end it all with fifty aspirin from Harrods.

If Penelope wrote semi-autobiographically, as she stated, then both stories certainly disclose something of the reality lurking behind the façade (but also, seemingly, that she had some sympathy with her beleaguered husband). She could see that she was inventing characters based on John, using writing to 'get rid of my scorn for some aspects of men in general', but still insistent that none of her characters had John's positive qualities, his talent, fun, charm and sexual attraction. She was to maintain that she never wrote directly about herself, although acknowledging that all of her women protagonists were victims of insensitive husbands, financially secure, did not work outside the home, and (a surprising statement from Penelope) did not much enjoy their children.

John was again straying, and in 1958 came Penelope's fourth published novel, the blistering *Daddy's Gone A-Hunting*, in which a depressed middle-aged mother of three, Ruth, is trapped in the home while her selfish husband philanders in London. She badly misses her sons who – thanks to their father – are away at boarding school. The narrative centres around the secret abortion she must arrange for her adult daughter (just as Penelope herself had been obliged to do for one of hers), and the obstruction and disgust she meets with in her attempts: 'You would really advise her to do this thing? Your own daughter? Good God Ruth, I'm sorry. You make me sick,' protests the family doctor. The novel received excellent reviews and is very moving in its depiction of a mother's feelings: Penelope's writing was often to reflect her true love and understanding of children, despite occasional frustrations.

In the final year of the 1950s Penelope suffered a miscarriage. The older children were starting to leave home, the house seemed empty and John was catching up on all he had missed, which as far as Penelope could see meant having a string of girlfriends. He wanted Penelope's blessing to all this, but she was unable to give it, and felt contempt for him. By now very unhappy, she lived for the short, hectic bouts of reconciliation in between the affairs but always, in her own words, there ran through everything she did (except her writing) 'an undercurrent of apprehension and mourning'.

In 1961, discovering that she was pregnant for the eighth time at the age of forty-two, Penelope felt contentment: to have another baby would be 'comforting'. But her doctor advised a termination in light of her age and because of her previous miscarriage. John, too, wanted an abortion – and sterilisation – on the grounds that yet another baby would make their future life together difficult, perhaps impossible. Penelope chose to believe in the idea of a happy future still married to John and went ahead with the operation, afterwards even feeling somewhat relieved. She then discovered that all along John had been having another affair, with actress Wendy Craig.

She had been 'tricked into permanent loss', she realised. Devastated, Penelope was prescribed the anti-depressant Cavodil, a drug which made her feel 'half dead and quite uncertain' (and which was shortly afterwards withdrawn by the manufacturers because of its toxic effect on the liver). She wrote in her diary:

Being pregnant, aborted, sterilised, wounded – it's not surprising, I know, that nothing heals. 'Involutionary depression' I read, but don't know what it means. All I want is for it to be over.

For the family's sake some sort of normality was achieved but, inside, Penelope remained hugely angry. John's reaction to her hurt was to turn against her, calling her hideous and useless. But, although she did not yet know it, 'extreme despair is often the final stage of gestation'. That November, on the exact day she had married her first husband almost a quarter of a century before, Penelope began to write *The Pumpkin Eater,* her celebrated story of a betrayed wife and mother. The opening words 'lit up the dark corners of my heart' as she wrote them.

A few days later Wendy Craig gave birth to John's son. John claimed to have discovered the existence of this son only many years afterwards (unlikely).

§

Penelope took her title from the nursery rhyme:

> *Peter, Peter pumpkin eater,*
> *Had a wife but couldn't keep her;*
> *He put her in a pumpkin shell*
> *And there he kept her very well.*

Mrs Armitage (never given a first name) is the mother of a large brood; some, from previous marriages, have been sent away to boarding school with money from her father, who thinks this will be better for her present husband Jake; she is left desolate and burning with anger. Jake, a newly successful scriptwriter, provides his wife with so much household help – staff to do the housekeeping and a nanny to look after the children – that she is left alienated and without purpose. After a breakdown in Harrods, crying and sprinkling bolts of cloth with her tears (based on a real event in Penelope's life), she is sent to a psychiatrist. He prescribes pills to 'pep you up a little', but Mrs Armitage remains unhappy, conscious that Jake is unfaithful. She tries to understand Jake's own frustrations but then deliberately becomes pregnant yet again – possibly to give her life new meaning – while knowing her husband is against it. Jake argues for a freer future together and talks her into an abortion and sterilisation.

While recovering in the hospital, Mrs Armitage discovers that Jake has been having an affair and her operation wound immediately gapes open, as though laughing at her. Jake denies everything but in a horrible scene slowly admits the truth. She asks how many others there have been:

There weren't any others!

How many?

I've told you! None!

How many?

Half a dozen. A dozen. I don't know. What does it matter, how many?

The Pumpkin Eater, Penelope Mortimer, 1962

Somehow they patch things up and life goes on – until Mrs Armitage learns that Jake's mistress is pregnant. She flees to a former husband and then takes refuge in a tower she and Jake have been building in the country. After three days her husband and the children come looking for her, Jake bringing up the rear as the children converge and surround the tower to prevent her escape. The novel ends as Mrs Armitage, finally accepting Jake as he is, allows him into the tower, with the bleak implication that the marriage will continue.

The Pumpkin Eater, published in 1962, was revolutionary at the time in its depiction of marital discord. Because it is in the first person the novel is extremely immediate, as though happening there and then to the reader. Mrs Armitage's life, from youth to her present predicament, is slowly revealed in fragments during therapy sessions with her psychiatrist, and much of the rest of the novel is dialogue too. It is witty – 'You really should have been an Inquisitor,' Mrs Armitage says to the psychiatrist, 'Do I burn now, or later?' – and beautifully written: 'I want to fly from a window and pour through the air like a wind of love to raise his hair and slide into the palms of his hands,' she mourns after leaving her still-loved husband. It is occasionally also somewhat obscure, however: Penelope was a great believer in writer Raymond Chandler's maxim that scarcely anything in literature is worth a damn except what is written between the lines, but in Penelope's case this can be unclear:

I was worrying about the milk, about my children falling in love, about the creatures who crawled through the dark towards us, their ancestors, their loving assassins, breathing 'Why?' like a cold wind.

The Pumpkin Eater, Penelope Mortimer, 1962

In a BBC television programme in 1963 she cast further light on the meaning of the novel, and perhaps thereby herself, by explaining that Jake is not mature enough to cope with the amount of money he is newly earning, while Mrs Armitage is shielded from reality by her swarm of children. Jake's affairs with other women mean nothing to him but destroy her, said Penelope, because she has no confidence in her own existence without him and without the children. (She is perhaps only 'Mrs Armitage' because she has no identity beyond that of wife: 'I don't know who I am, I don't know what I'm like,' she states disconsolately.)

Clearly, *The Pumpkin Eater* is as close to autobiography as a novel can be and still call itself fiction. While her central character is not a novelist like Penelope the details certainly mirror a great deal of her personal experience, although the extent to which the generally unpleasant Jake is a reflection of John Mortimer cannot be known (even if according to Penelope's memoirs John did, like Jake, ask why didn't Penelope just *die*, a line which gets more or less repeated in the subsequent film). Despite the autobiographical element, however, Penelope did mean it to have a more general application. 'I have put into this novel practically everything I can say about men and women and their relationship to one another,' she said of her most famous work. As Mrs Armitage observes at the close of the novel,

Some of these things happened, and some were dreams. They are all true, as I understood truth. They are all real, as I understood reality.

The Pumpkin Eater, Penelope Mortimer, 1962

§

When Penelope opened the *Express* to read the first, glowing review she was horrified to see that the centre-page spread included an account of her problems with depression, and she rushed off to be repeatedly sick. Once that had passed, though, her daughter Caroline (the actress Caroline Mortimer) remembered Penelope carolling out 'I'm a genius! I'm a genius!'. Reviews were indeed glittering. 'Almost every woman I can think of will want to read this book,' said fellow novelist Edna O'Brien. For the *Times* the work was the best she had written, her technique unobtrusive, her language pliant but exact, her imagery poetic 'but so accurate it looks down-to-earth'. For the *Telegraph* it was a 'shattering achievement'. *The Pumpkin Eater* was a 'beautifully compact, effortlessly readable novel,' said the *Tatler*, and its author wrote with a very sharp eye. Across the Atlantic, the *New York Times* wrote that it was 'a subtle, fascinating, unhackneyed novel' and that 'Mrs Mortimer is tough-minded, in touch with human realities and frailties, unsentimental and amused. Her prose is deft and precise. A fine book, and one to be greatly enjoyed.'

John Mortimer, to his credit, thought the novel 'brilliant' – according to Penelope, at least. He professed to admire his wife for writing it (and as he himself frequently used their life together as fodder for his own fiction, he could hardly object). It might be supposed that he would fear some personal criticism, but in fact he knew that not many outside the family would be aware how truthful the work was. His public comment was that he never felt the book to be any kind of revenge, or that Jake was meant to be him. 'When I read it, all I thought was that it was a very good book.'

The success of *The Pumpkin Eater* was naturally very pleasing to Penelope, although she maintained she couldn't understand it and had no wish to be taken up by the literary establishment, who were keen to do so. Not long after publication she received a telegram from her friend Jack Clayton, director of the big film hit *Room at the Top*. 'Dear Penelope,' he wrote. 'After months of soul searching have come to the foolish decision that I can make as ghastly a film out of your ghastly book as anyone else.' She accepted the offer.

Penelope was considered as screenwriter, but, apparently finding her wanting, Jack Clayton gave the job of writing the script to playwright Harold Pinter – sometimes labelled an 'Angry Young Man' himself – who was fortunately a writer loved and admired by Penelope. Beautiful American actress Anne Bancroft played the main role and was forever after associated with the film, although not Jack Clayton's first choice. He had considered both Deborah Kerr and Ingrid Bergman for the part of Mrs Armitage, now christened Jo in the screenplay, but neither was the right age. Deborah was British and would certainly have been a more natural choice than Bronx-born Anne, but in her early forties she was a decade older than Anne while Ingrid was older by a full sixteen years. After reading the novel Anne felt deeply about the character and cabled Clayton that she was the only one who could play the role. On Jack's request, she sent stills from her recent hit movie *The Miracle Worker* (about deaf and blind Helen Keller) and then turned up in London in person. Jack, struck by her beauty, was immediately convinced, but with one condition: that she spend a month in Britain learning the accent. Anne agreed. She made good progress and claimed to be able to fool shop assistants up until the point she was forced to spread the baffling pounds, shillings and pence across the counter for help in deciphering British currency. 'I can speak with the accent,' she said, 'but I'll never understand British money.'

Jack Clayton asked a clutch of psychiatrists to read Pinter's script and provide an analysis of Jo Armitage for his leading lady. The diagnosis was of a neurotic hysteric unable to square her romantic fantasies with reality and as a consequence suffering reactive depression, the type of clinical depression experienced after stressful life events. Anne commented in interviews that there was something 'depressingly universal' about Jo's problems: she had everything and yet nothing, and it could have happened to her too. She played the part very believably, and movingly, with impeccable British accent and exquisitely applied eyeliner throughout and, in good Sixties fashion, smoking during pregnancy. The famous scene of the breakdown in Harrods' Food Hall is painful to watch (although to some, overdone, and in the words of critic Michael Billington carrying overtones of privileged despair, as if it were inherently more tragic than a nervous collapse in Safeway's).

Peter Finch took the role of Jake, interpreting the character as a fundamentally decent man and good father trying to do the best he can with his depressive wife and too numerous brood. A youthful Maggie Smith was a prattling girl in love with Jake, and James Mason was the vengeful husband of Jake's mistress. Throughout the film Jo's many children babble and play, a crucial source of meaning and atmosphere – sometimes signifying life and the future, other times becoming a distraction or irritation or the focus of the battle between their parents.

Harold Pinter in his screenplay mostly kept to Penelope's original dialogue, although sharpening some of it to achieve his characteristic terseness, and inserting his equally characteristic pauses and silences. He also introduced entirely new episodes such as the one in which a woman seated next to Mrs Armitage at the hairdresser's turns abusive – a menacing yet comic scene played to the hilt by *Man About the House* actress Yootha Joyce, and described by Penelope as 'ghoulish' and 'vintage Pinter'.

Director Jack Clayton kept to the central plot of the novel: a woman isolated from her children because the eldest have been sent to boarding school and a nanny employed for the youngest, and then forced into abortion and sterilisation by a husband who is betraying her with another woman. But he cut and modified some of Harold's script – ruining it, in the opinion of one academic. These additions and changes to the storyline, and the upright way Peter Finch played Jake, meant that the characters and their behaviour in the film became 'almost unrecognisable' to Penelope. There were also omissions: to her great annoyance, scenes from the novel implying that in Jo's girlhood a precocious schoolfriend may have seduced Jo's loving, honourable father, had simply been left out. To her mind this lost a crucial point respecting a valuable early lesson about life – presumably meaning the faithlessness of men or the seduction of men by women – that Jo should have learned from:

The underlying story of childhood, which I thought essential, was intended to illustrate that those who cannot remember experience are condemned to repeat it...it was just a simple assumption that you can't have an effect without a cause. All this was considered unnecessary to the movie.

In addition, Penelope complained, the throng of children in the novel had been reduced in the film to just three stolid, well-behaved offspring and a silent toddler (in fact the film did firmly establish that there were six), while Mrs Armitage was dressed in designer clothing and photographed in artistic lighting:

There was Miss Bancroft with her hats and her silk lampshades and matching china – I mean, these people were supposed to be careless, and <u>suddenly</u> rich.

Seeing Anne Bancroft married to the mostly decent Peter Finch, Penelope now couldn't see what Mrs Armitage had to complain about. But her main gripe, as she passionately relayed to Harold Pinter, was the anticlimactic ending. In the book the mother flees to her tower on a hill but is tracked down and captured by her numberless brood while husband Jake lets them do the catching, knowing that this is the only way to get her back. In the film it is brave Peter Finch who breasts the hill in search of his wife with what Penelope termed the 'mingy' family coming up behind, and Mrs Armitage is brought docilely back into the fold with an offer of a can of beer.

Penelope had been kept at arm's length during the shooting, which she had reluctantly accepted, although sometimes meeting secretly with Harold for discussions. After hearing her stinging critique of the final product he sent her a copy of the script with 'I'm sorry' written across it. But with the passing of time Penelope was able to accept that the film had style, and that it may have had something to say to the English middle classes about themselves, 'if not about human nature'.

The film, in black and white, opened at Cannes just at the point the novel was topping the paperback bestseller list. French critics at Cannes were baffled and even outraged by the behaviour of its very middle-class English characters, but granted Anne Bancroft their Best Actress Award. Harold Pinter also won a British Film Academy award for the best screenplay of 1964, while Anne Bancroft further won a Golden Globe Award and the BAFTA Award for Best Foreign Actress. She was additionally nominated for an Oscar (losing, incongruously, to Julie Andrews in *Mary Poppins*). The Film Critics' Guild voted *The Pumpkin Eater* Film of the Year. It was subsequently 'tightened' by its editor and the result, in the view of celebrated film critic Alexander Walker, was one of the best films ever made.

Some film critics were more ambivalent, though mostly in agreement that Anne Bancroft was superb, if a bit given or directed towards long, despairing gazes into space. For the *Times* the scene showing a knockdown fight between the Armitages – a 45-second brawl which took nearly three days to film, and during which Peter Finch professed to be frightened by Anne Bancroft's aggression – and another scene displaying increasingly large close-ups of James Mason's crooked teeth as he reveals the story of his wife's affair with Jake to Mrs Armitage, were 'quite embarrassingly inept'. The *New York Times* dubbed Miss Bancroft's performance 'over-agonized' and her parade of melancholy expressions monotonous, while James Mason was dismissed as testy but trifling. In Australia the *Canberra Times*, however, thought Anne Bancroft played her part with 'blood-curdling magnificence' (and saw her as possessed of such 'sheer animal femininity' that her aura of sexuality surpassed that of many more highly touted sex goddesses). 'A devastating experience', observed *Maclean's* magazine in Canada, too much of it superficially clever, but nevertheless setting an interesting precedent for a more truthful treatment of women in the movies.

For other critics the pristine fashion-magazine home of the Armitages was hardly credible as the habitation of a swarm of children, nor elegant Anne Bancroft as mother of the same. The *Times Literary Supplement* wrote that Harold Pinter had not properly tackled the problem of adapting a first-person narrative, in which all the action and characters are seen through the eyes of a woman undergoing a nervous breakdown, to action which is seen from the outside (and indeed both Pinter and Jack Clayton did struggle with this); and that Pinterish scenes such as the one at the hairdresser's with Yootha Joyce were merely 'decorative excrescences'. As for the dialogue, their review continued, while good in itself it seemed disconnected from director Jack Clayton's 'would-be objective,

Antonioni-esque cool'. This was not the only reference to Clayton's supposed emulation of Italian director Antonioni, chronicler of Italy's anxious and idle rich. One review was actually entitled 'Keeping Up with the Antonionis' and implied that *The Pumpkin Eater* was nothing but a cheap copy of the style.

Jo Armitage as the main character attracted particular criticism. The British Film Institute's *Monthly Film Bulletin* thought the film absurd, with Jo such a humourless, crashing bore that it was hard to see why her husband had any love for her at all. It was like a two-hour thunderstorm, the reviewer commented, with plenty of lightning but barely a drop of rain to refresh or lead to growth. The *Illustrated London News* was in agreement, finding the film over-praised and Mrs Armitage an 'unredeemably tiresome type'. Why didn't she learn a language, read the classics or otherwise occupy her mind – if indeed she had one? The *Tatler* critic, meanwhile, suspected that the male trio of screenwriter, producer and director had rather less sympathy for the beautiful heroine than her creator Penelope Mortimer. A father stuck with so many brats, only one of which he has fathered, was in the critic's view entitled to lose patience with a wife who took no interest in his profession, refused to go on work trips abroad with him and was naggingly jealous. All this from a woman obsessed with having children but who seemed not to bother with any of them once she had had the pleasure of producing them, the review concluded sourly.

As for audiences, they appeared bemused as to the exact nature of Jo's problems and what the film was actually about, perhaps because of Peter Finch's portrayal of Jake as an essentially upright man, despite the philandering. They were not alone: Harold Pinter described the film (tersely) as 'about marriage' while director Jack Clayton confusingly explained it as dealing with 'the infinitely simple idea of the difficulties in any married relationship while at the same time showing the tremendously strong relationship that grows almost inevitably' (adding that the film might be prejudiced and one-sided). In Canada *Maclean's* magazine opted for 'how the world looks to a woman battling against the chaos of life with the only weapon at her disposal – her ability to have children'. One film critic described it as 'Mrs Armitage experiences serious anxiety brought on by her relationship with her remote father'. Writer Elaine Dundy, in her biography of actor Peter Finch, gave another tortuous description: that the film was about the plight of a woman in love with a man who is dissatisfied with himself whom she is unable either to help or to resist, and although blaming herself is just beginning to suspect that it is not entirely her fault. A much later review safely covered all the bases with the comment that it was 'a remarkably honest film about love, sex, marriage, infidelity, reproduction and parenthood'. For the respected drama critic Michael Billington it was a feminist film, one filled with dismay at the abysmal failure of men to understand women's needs and desires, and one of the first post-war British films to treat a specifically feminine problem with any degree of seriousness. As for the famous film critic Pauline Kael, *The Pumpkin Eater* was 'a remarkable study of modern sexual tensions'.

The film was not a financial success, constrained in part at the American box office by its status as an art film, although faring better in Britain and Europe. It is rarely screened today. Anne Bancroft went on to achieve cult status playing another memorable mother of the 1960s, one Mrs Robinson in *The Graduate*.

§

Not long after *The Pumpkin Eater* came out Penelope made another suicide attempt, again by overdose. The newspapers reported her arrival at hospital in a coma and John commented publicly that his wife had been receiving treatment for insomnia 'and must have taken a few pills too many'. She was later subjected to the traumatic procedure of electroconvulsive therapy, in which small electric currents are passed through the brain in an attempt to cure depression.

The marriage with John did not last, dissolving into unsurprising acrimony. 'You're useless as a wife and extremely unpleasant as a companion,' Mortimer reportedly flung at Penelope, also joking nastily that whenever Penelope thought things were getting dull she would tell another daughter who her real father was. As for Penelope, she too had carried on affairs during the marriage, including with the playwright David Mercer. She and John divorced in 1971, with Penelope stating to the court that living with him was intolerable because of his adultery. John offered no defence, and indeed had already had the first of two children with his soon-to-be second wife (the child grew up to be actress Emily Mortimer). He became more and more celebrated, particularly for his TV and book series *Rumpole of the Bailey* – whose terrifying wife was known as She Who Must Be Obeyed – but Penelope's star slowly faded. She continued to produce novels (increasingly, about women on their own), wrote screenplays, and went several times to America to teach creative writing, but eventually retreated to live alone in a cottage in the Cotswolds where her passion turned to gardening. Her beautiful garden was to feature in a 1987 coffee table book about gardens of the rich and famous.

She did not remarry or find love again, although there were a number of relationships. According to Penelope there was a proposal of marriage from film director Clive Donner, which she turned down. Interestingly, Clive introduced her to *Georgy Girl* author Margaret Forster, whose husband Hunter Davies had written the novel of one of Clive's films, and the two couples spent an awkward evening together. Penelope and Clive seemed wrong for each other, Margaret thought, 'such a contrast, with Clive so soft and limp, and Penelope so stern and full of suppressed fury'.

For a long time Penelope found it difficult to fully let go of the relationship with John, who was always to bask happily in his reputation as a womaniser. About the last throes of their marriage she wrote:

...it was as though all my sexual impulses had been conditioned to respond to one particular stimulus and that, for better (he was my husband) or worse (he was an unsatisfactory husband), was John. I longed for something, someone, to rid me of this disability. A number of men would try, and as many psychiatrists...Perhaps a woman might have been the answer, but I was far too timid to venture into a different world and violently rejected any invitation to do so.

In 1973 she had a hysterectomy and suffered more deep depression. Life remained a struggle: she was unable to make sense of her new self, neither wife nor potential mother. She felt she no longer knew who she was:

The outside world identified me as 'ex-wife of John Mortimer, mother of six, author of The Pumpkin Eater' – accurate, as far as it went, but to me unrecognisable.

She died at the age of 81.

§

Today Penelope is chiefly known for *The Pumpkin Eater*, republished as a Penguin Classic in 2015, while the rest of her novels are mostly out of print. Over time the novel has been taken more and more seriously, both as good writing – a 'stinging little novel', said the discerning critic Peter Hitchens in 2016 – and very often as an early feminist tract anticipating milestones such as Betty Friedan's imminent *Feminine Mystique*, as highlighted by the *Guardian* in its 2015 re-examination of Penelope's work. 'She captured the times every bit as deftly as any angry young man,' declared the article, 'dealing with what [Friedan] would call "the problem with no name": the madness that was born of being a certain kind of wife, with a certain kind of husband; of the suffocating feeling that life was going on elsewhere.'

Feminist elements are certainly there: the tedium and confinement of domestic life make themselves felt in the novel, and were frequently much resented by Penelope in actuality. 'My life has been measured out in meals, socks, little bloody Noddy', she wrote in her diary only a few weeks before starting work on *The Pumpkin Eater*. And Mrs Armitage is certainly angry at the world's attitude to the female sex:

A womb isn't all that important. It's only the seat of life...At school the word 'womb' used to make them snigger. Women aren't important.

The Pumpkin Eater, Penelope Mortimer, 1962

But Penelope herself, when asked by director Jack Clayton what the novel was actually about, did not refer to feminist angst as its raison d'être. Her response was surprising: money. Money as a theme does make sense.

121

Mrs Armitage is deprived of her older sons when her father's money is used to send them away to boarding school, and of her other children when Jake's money is used to hire a nanny and household help. Jake accuses his wife of resenting his money after he has become a successful screenwriter and, in Penelope's own words, he is not mature enough himself to cope with the amount of money he is newly earning. But Penelope then wrote to Jack to amplify her answer as to the ultimate meaning of the work:

It boils down to the conflict between and the fusion of reality and fantasy; and perhaps what results from some kind of uneasy balance between the two. It's also about money (and success); love (and sex and hate); and the creation of children.

To view *The Pumpkin Eater* as a feminist tirade expressing only resentment at patriarchy and the frustrations of motherhood is to ignore these clearly stated layers. Mrs Armitage may sometimes feel maddened by domesticity but she also feels Penelope's own compulsion to have children, and loves them deeply in the same way. She takes obvious pleasure in a home awash with life and noise and Wellington boots, and like Penelope is bereft and angry when robbed of it by the imposition of boarding schools and nannies that take her children away from her. Motherhood, despite its shackles, gives meaning to life, as expressed in her earlier novel *Daddy's Gone A-Hunting*: people might moan about being impeded by children, she wrote, but

...without them, life would be too dangerous; an emptiness in which, the most fearful thing of all, there would be no time, no landmarks.

Daddy's Gone A-Hunting, Penelope Mortimer, 1958

Yes, Penelope Mortimer was angry when she wrote *The Pumpkin Eater*, angry at the loss, through faithlessness, of the immensely significant home and family.

Up the Junction and Poor Cow

Nell Dunn

You've got to be careful sometimes, it's as if I'm hanging on all the time – just clinging on telling meself – life's all right – it's a great experience living – look at all the different people yer meeting – you really are living and then I think, Poor Cow, who are you taking on? Let's face it, it's just escaping from one misery to another. Who really enjoys life? Kids when you get down to it – kids are the only ones who really get a kick out of being alive...

Poor Cow, Nell Dunn, 1967

Nell Dunn is a descendant of Charles II, the daughter of a baronet and granddaughter of the 5th Earl of Rosslyn. Her sister married a Rothschild.

A surprising background for the writer of the very raw, working-class narratives *Up the Junction* and *Poor Cow*. Born in London in 1936 to businessman Sir Philip Dunn – son of a wealthy Canadian steel magnate – and his wife Lady Mary Sybil St Clair-Erskine, Nell was the second of two daughters. As a three-year-old she was evacuated to America for the early part of the war and she and her older sister, Serena, returned in 1943 to find their parents on the point of separation. Her mother and father each bought a farm in Wiltshire and the girls divided their time between the two parents, soon learning to ride and care for animals and do the work of a farm; they were free to run about and were encouraged to be independent. Trips to London happened rarely, and as a country girl Nell learned to look on the city as a place of excitement where she herself was just an observer.

Education was at a convent boarding school, which Nell loved for its quiet orderliness and familiar routine, but at the age of fourteen she was taken away: her father Sir Philip disliked overly educated women and did not believe his daughters needed any qualifications. Formal education reduced people to the same level, he maintained, and he and his wife wanted their daughters to be cultured and individual. This early departure from the convent meant that Nell never passed a single exam her entire life, although she was always to read widely. Sir Philip would laugh at her appalling spelling, but not unkindly – for Nell, his laugh carried the message that she was a completely original person and everything she did had her own mark on it. 'He wanted us all to be unique,' she said. Her father also conveyed another message to his children: that life was for enjoyment. 'You dressed for pleasure, you ate for pleasure,' Nell summed up. 'What has stayed with me is the knowledge that pleasure exists and that it is absolutely the thing to aim for.'

Nell's beautiful mother, Lady Mary, was well travelled and a talented linguist but, according to her daughter, elusive and self-centred – although benignly so. She too believed her girls should go their own way and have fun, just as she used to do herself at horse races and film premieres when a young woman. Family life with two such parents was 'bohemian', as Nell put it, despite the employment of nannies to care for them (one of whom once locked the two girls alone in a bathroomless New York hotel room where, according to Nell, they had to hold one another out of the thirtieth-floor window to relieve themselves).

Nell, unsurprisingly, was not brought up to follow conventional strictures. 'I was never told any rules and I suppose I absorbed some which were to do with somehow keeping one's head high on some level, somehow finding some dignity.' After leaving the convent as a young teenager she was packed off for finishing in Europe; in Rome, with little grasp of Italian, she took refuge in reading, perfectly happy with her own company but relieved to have other English girls to talk to at a subsequent establishment in Paris. Returning to England at the age of seventeen, she was launched into society by her mother, the *Sketch* society paper describing the young heiress as inheritor of Lady Mary's 'piquante good looks'. Sensitive about her lack of qualifications, Nell found that other people – particularly middle-class people – enjoyed making her feel inferior for her want of proper education. This, she was to say, gave her 'a great and immediate empathy with the working class, many of whom were anti-education. I have always been drawn to the company of the intelligent uneducated.'

Her father knew the head of the Courtauld Institute of Art (and Soviet spy) Anthony Blunt, and by this back door means secured the totally ineligible Nell a place on a history of art course, but she left in 1957 to marry and have a baby. The groom was eccentric author and old Etonian Jeremy Sandford. 'I fell for a rich girl because I think money in girls is sexy and glamorous,' he was to comment. 'They can do what they want. They're not scheming. Middle-class girls are just whores, selling themselves for security.' After the Catholic ceremony at St Patrick's in Soho Square the reception at the Ritz was reported in the press as 'one of London's craziest weddings', with Jeremy playing the piano while he and Nell sang *Ain't Misbehavin'* and *Two Sleepy People* for their guests. Plans to depart for the honeymoon in a hot air balloon had been abandoned after objections from the Ministry of Works; a Movietone news item showed Nell leaving the Ritz rather more conventionally by car, elegantly arrayed in 1950s going-away outfit of flowered sleeveless dress and lampshade hat.

In 1959 Nell and Jeremy and their young son left their five-storey house in Chelsea's upmarket Cheyne Walk (a present from their parents) to go and live in the shadow of Battersea Power Station. Heiress Nell was ultimately to decide, and perhaps had already done so at this point, that she did not want to inherit the family money or live in a grand way. 'I never, ever wanted a conventional life and big house,' she was to declare later. 'I always wanted a lot of freedom.' Living in Cheyne Walk she had felt very lost, and 'rather scared' by the river. The neighbours objected to her hanging washing out, and there was no one to talk to on walks with the baby. She took to strolling over the bridge to Battersea, where people would gather round the pram and talk to her; she liked them, and realised that she felt happier there. She saw a two-up, two-down cottage for sale for £700, with a big garden full of sunflowers and a grapevine growing wild over the outdoor toilet. They decided to buy it and live over the river.

§

Battersea was then more or less a slum, but people kept rabbits and pigeons in the back gardens and sat on their doorsteps on hot summer evenings enjoying their fish and chips. The street after street of Victorian houses seemed very pretty to Nell, and she even loved the bomb sites and gangs of stray dogs, and Battersea Power Station with its early morning plumes of mauve smoke drifting up into the sky. She and Jeremy fitted the cottage with a bathroom, the first in the street, and soon new friends were coming round for the unfamiliar treat of a bath – to wash at home they had to fill a plastic bowl with water and take it up to their tiny back bedrooms, keeping their dirty feet till last – and to try on Nell's and each other's clothes. It was a highly spontaneous, friendly way of life, Nell remembered. The women she was getting to know were just as interested in Nell, with her cut-glass tones, as she was in them.

It was so different, it was like arriving in Mexico. I felt happy and relaxed straight away...I prefer working-class people. You can get to the bottom of things, people tell the truth. When you move into a new street you're important, everybody gapes, wants to know who you are, says hello, looks at your babies. In a place like Chelsea, you're just ignored.

She knew that this was all very well and that she had the security of money behind her and could move out whenever she wanted. But she didn't want to. She was perfectly serious about her new life south of the river. Some of the locals, of course, soon understood that the couple had money, and the cottage was a target for burglars on at least one occasion.

In those years there was plenty of work and if the girls Nell now knew lost a job 'through cheek or pilfering' they could easily move on to another, and the same with boyfriends. The girls were quite feminist in a way, Nell remembered – 'they wouldn't put up with a lot'. When Nell's son was old enough for nursery she went to work alongside them in a sweet factory, where she used a hot rod to draw cellophane across boxes of liqueur chocolates for 2/5d an hour. It was fun, she recalled later, lots of chat and jokes and camaraderie, although conceding that unlike the rest of the girls she only worked part time for two or three hours a day. They were allowed to eat as many of the sweets as they wanted (which soon palled), and because they contained real whisky some of the girls would get drunk.

She had her hair bleached blonde and done in a beehive, wore skin-tight white jeans from the market and went for rides on the back of boys' motorbikes like the other girls. She always felt welcomed, never an interloper, and was far more comfortable in an environment which took her back to a childhood of being cared for by working-class people. A bit of her wanted to remain in that childhood state, Nell recognised, and not grow up and deal with the real world. She also just liked the people more. 'I suppose there was something about warming myself with these working-class relationships which are so immediate and verbal and present, rather than the remote and spacious relationships of my own background,' she commented when looking back. Some of the girls she worked with were labelled slags by the others for their free and easy approach to their love lives, but they had 'marvellous energy', in Nell's words. 'God knows, if most girls lived up to their standards, the world would be a gayer place.'

Excited by the escape from her moneyed background to the energy of Battersea, Nell eventually began to write stories based on the lives of the girls around her. She had been inspired by a 1959 television documentary, *Morning in the Streets* by Dennis Mitchell, described at the time as an 'impression of life and opinion in the backstreets of a Northern City'. This innovative film was a mix of observational and staged scenes, with occasional floating snatches of recorded conversation, and was just the sort of thing Nell wanted to write. She arranged to meet the author on a platform at Clapham Junction station, where they sat and talked on a bench. Dennis Mitchell was encouraging (they never again met) and the pieces Nell then produced were to contribute to her collection *Up the Junction*. The title referred to the area around the station but was also an echo of the then current slang phrase 'up the duff', for being pregnant.

Previous attempts at writing had been rejected and she was increasingly anxious to get published:

I wanted to be a writer and I'd written journals, but I hadn't quite seen how to tie things together. And so I began to write a portrait of Battersea, really. There's about five years of living in Battersea that's distilled into Up the Junction.

Her English teacher at the convent had given her the classics to read and encouraged her to write; her first play, written with great zest at the age of eleven or twelve, was about cannibals. However, she was always frank about her own failings in the field. 'I'm fairly uneducable,' she admitted. 'I can't spell. My mother and grandmother had the same disorganised minds. I have a very good memory for what I hear and see and a not particularly good memory for word experience or word learning.' This instinctive ear for dialogue was better with women than with men, but if Nell heard somebody talking for a day or two she could then almost speak in their voice and write that person into a situation using their own natural expression. All her dialogue was overheard speech, Nell later clarified, 'but I put it in different patterns and I string it on a different thread.' She also said that all of her characters were part her and part other people, and while she might be speaking in what was seen as working-class language she was actually saying what she herself thought.

There was another reason for her writing ambitions. As a young girl she had realised that men were the important ones and that women were seen as rather boring: to have 'housewife' on your passport meant no status, no glamour, Nell had seen. Now she wanted to achieve something.

Her talent was finally recognised. The left-wing magazine *New Statesman* began to publish some of her pieces, showing her how to pare them down into the lean, simple language that suited them. Nell found it all immensely exciting and she would read out sections of her frank tales to the factory girls who had lived them, which they enjoyed and did not find shocking. A publisher then contacted her to suggest putting her stories together in a book and *Up the Junction* came out in 1963, a collection of roughly connected pieces about the lives of young men and women in Battersea.

The girls and women in *Up the Junction* work in sweet factory or butter factory, go out at night and pick up boys, buy clothes 'off the barrers', take prams laden with washing to the public baths, and pay – or try to evade paying – the Tally Man for their new underwear and bedroom suites bought on instalment. In one story Sylvie squats behind a truck to relieve herself and the truck drives off. 'Here, wait till I've pulled me drawers up!' she shouts. In another, girls in a home for unmarried mothers talk about sex and a black girl is delivered of a (maybe) stillborn baby and then is never seen again. Ruby has an agonising, illegal abortion brought on by a backstreet abortionist using a syringe, a procedure which has to be repeated on seven different occasions before taking effect. She suffers through the birth at home, refusing to have the doctor called in case he tries to save the baby. The five-month-old foetus is born breathing but soon dies, and is wrapped in a *Daily Mirror* and flushed down the toilet.

The boys work in scrapyards or cleaning windows, go thieving, ride their motorbikes and cheat on the wives they married too young. Rube's boyfriend Terry collides with a lorry, is thrown from his motorbike and dies on the road, the back wheel of the smashed bike still spinning. A husband and wife fight each other in the street outside the pub, the wife's mother arriving in a nightdress to weigh in on behalf of her daughter. The book ends poignantly, with a group of dirty, bare-legged children playing on waste land where cranes are clearing the slums for the high-rise flats signalling the end of the old community. A young girl, legs skinny under her velvet dress, takes her five-year-old brother by the hand to get him out of the rain; watching them go the reader understands, although the children do not, that the old ways are disappearing for ever.

The existence described is bleak and hopeless but the book simply pulses with life, the stories of young and old alike told mostly through long passages of ripe dialogue. Pop music of the Sixties plays both as a backdrop and as indirect, often ironic commentary on the action – Ben E King's *Ecstasy* thrumming on a juke box in a dirty café, Sam Cooke's *Twistin' the Night Away* drumming out as the girls take their break at the factory, Rube singing *He's Got the Power* by the Exciters after an afternoon doing washing at the baths. Much of the action plays out on the streets of South London, in rain or shine:

The builders from the new flats whistle as we go past the corner shop – nylon film panties one-and-three pegged between the tinned peas and plastic toys – arm in arm with the sun jumping off the pavement.

Great gusts of black smoke blow sideways out of the four chimneys of Fulham gasworks across a streaky sky.

Down the street women stand at their doors and two young girls walk hippity-hop on their high heels eating fish and chips.

Up the Junction, Nell Dunn, 1963

The unnamed narrator, the 'I' of most of the stories, is clearly Nell. 'She's an heiress from Chelsea,' one of her friends introduces her. Like Nell apparently fully accepted in her new milieu, she too works in a factory but is also sometimes in what seems like journalistic, fact-gathering mode, working as a temporary hostess at a clip joint – a club, on occasion a front for prostitution, which offered adult entertainment and where the customers were tricked into paying high prices for drinks – or accompanying the duplicitous Tally Man on his rounds. The narrator seemingly witnesses both Rube's abortion (finally insisting on ringing for the doctor and the ambulance) and the death of Terry on his motorbike. She acts as a character witness at a boy's trial and goes along to visit him in prison. In fact, though, Nell later clarified that most of what she wrote in *Up the Junction* she either heard second-hand or invented – if clearly from close knowledge of the environment. Here are the girls setting off with the lads on their motorbikes to go swimming at night:

'Where we going?'

'Let's go swimmin' up the Common.'

'We ain't got no swim-suits with us.'

'We'll swim down one end and you down the other. It's dark, ain't it?'

'Who do yer think's going to see yer? The man in the moon?'

'Yeah and what's to stop yer hands wandering?'

'We'll tie 'em behind our backs.'

'Here, I'll never git on there, I can't get me knees apart.'

'Hitch yer skirt up under yer coat.'

'Help, me grandmother'll catch cold!'

There is no judgement in the book. The narrator simply records it all, leaving readers to be shocked or sympathetic as they see fit: the abortion, the robberies, the characters' casual racism. 'What you after, a bit of jungle juice?' Sylvie asks of a landlady who has taken in 'Coloureds'. Graffiti on a wall reads KEEP THE BLACKS OUT FOR A WHITE CHRISTMAS. The Tally Man thinks black people only have half the brain cells of whites, uses the 'n' word and tricks a gentle young immigrant into buying a cheap suit too small for him. (Ironically, the pop songs enjoyed by the youth of Battersea are mostly by black artistes.) However, it is telling that when the narrator herself refers to the immigrant she uses no racial terms but rather the accepted word at the time, 'Negro'.

The utterly astonishing *Up the Junction* was awarded the now defunct John Llewellyn Rhys Prize, then given annually for the best work of literature written in English by an author aged thirty-five or under. It became both a scandal and a runaway bestseller. Some critics positively raved. 'The real thing.' 'Remorseless observation.' 'A new and exciting young writer with an ear for the authentic idiom of the Smoke.' 'Razor quick, abrasive, hugely comic...'. The author managed to avoid any accusations of slumming for kicks or patronising her social inferiors because she abstained from the luxury of moral judgements, had a very accurate ear for racy spoken dialogue and genuinely loved Battersea, wrote *Anarchy* magazine. If there was any moral to be drawn, their critic continued, it was that people would go on enjoying life on their own terms and in their own way, despite ignorance, neglect or squalor, and would steadfastly resist being 'improved'. Nell's creation was 'a highly accomplished book, truthful and likeable,' approved the *Guardian* – although because of Nell's style of writing other critics saw it as mere reportage. '*Up the Junction* might have been called 'I am a Tape-recorder', wrote author David Lodge in the *Listener*. 'There is no attempt to weld the episodes into a novel...Miss Dunn's occasional attempts to create significance out of a pattern of events are not successful'.

The work's 'subject matter, its sexual frankness and its marked unsentimentality...its revelation of working class power – specially its portrayal of the forthrightness of working-class women, their strength, their unpretentious spirit – ignited a public reaction part scandalised, part ecstatic,' observed writer Ali Smith many decades later. The breakthrough radicalism of *Up the Junction* lay in to whom it gave voice as well as what it voiced, at a time when such things just weren't said, wrote Ali, continuing that Nell Dunn had a talent for hearing and relaying with uncanny authenticity the rhythms of idiom and that Nell was a pioneer, one of the clearest voices in the articulation and formation of change in social understanding about class and gender.

Local reaction was understandably one of shock.

I had a lot of people saying horrible things to me...They put letters through the letterbox saying, 'You've made all this horrible disgusting stuff up.' There was quite a strong class division in Battersea, and there was a sort of lower middle-class strata that thought that Up the Junction was quite a wicked book – because I'd made out that Battersea was full of 'wicked' people. It was a sort of non-recognition of things as they really were. I was really shocked because I thought it was exactly how things were.

§

The book was adapted into a television play by director of gritty dramas Ken Loach, then at the start of his directing career and working for the BBC. Ken had loved Nell's book and became desperate to direct it. 'It had a great sense of life, and a terrific energy,' he said. As with the novel, he wanted the play to be a kaleidoscope of fragmented images – the way real life happens, with plenty of loose ends rather than complete stories. He also desired an authentic capturing of working-class existence: 'raw, fleeting moments of people caught off guard', with the working-class characters not just playing bit parts as maids and taxi drivers but central to the story, and depicted without the usual condescension and caricature. With help from Nell on dialogue (most of it lifted straight from the book) he wrote a very simple adaptation of the stories but introduced characters who appear throughout, thus giving it more of a storyline. The 'Nell' narrator figure is dispensed with.

The November 1965 description of the forthcoming play in the *Radio Times*, written by assistant story editor Tony Garnett, was prophetic:

It is not a play, a documentary, or a musical. It is all of these at once. It is something new – but, more important, it is something true. If you watch it we can promise you something that will stay in your mind for a long time.

He wrote too of the exploitation in any big city in Britain, how so many were given a raw deal or just conveniently forgotten, and how in order to bring these still irrepressibly alive people to the screen he had instructed Ken that none of the sacred cows of television need stand in his way. The two of them, both from working-class backgrounds, had been 'moved and angered' by Nell's tale of youthful optimism in a grim environment. 'Ken and I had been allowed to escape,' Tony remarked. But there were battles to be fought to get the piece on screen as one of the BBC's hard-hitting *Wednesday Play* series. Knowing that the episodic, unconventional nature of the narrative might be too radical for their superiors, Ken and Tony started the project clandestinely behind the backs of a holidaying producer who would certainly not have allowed the kind of disjointed script Ken had come up with. Both were aware that if they reached a certain point in the process the play would have to air rather than leave a gap in programming. Then the producer returned. A huge row ensued, in fact a 'screaming match', as recalled by Tony, who threatened mass resignation if not allowed to proceed. Further struggle was to follow.

Both Ken and Tony wanted their Wednesday plays not to seem like invention, but to make them so lifelike that the audience would think it was actually happening (something that was to cause endless trouble and eventually, attempts to get them off the screen). This meant shooting in real locations and at the time the BBC was committed to drama shot only in the costly new studios at Television Centre. Tony successfully took on yet more of the corporation's management for permission to use 16mm cameras to go out and shoot on the streets, hoping this way to get the rough and raw immediacy of news footage. Then another problem loomed: the performers' union Equity insisted that 10% of any production must be shot in the studio. This stipulation Ken and Tony were unable to dodge, but managed to shoot the studio scenes in the same sort of style as the street action, with unplanned shots and the like that had technicians in an uproar.

In contravention of then BBC policy, therefore, a good half of the play was shot on location in the grimy streets of South London. Much of the action was improvised and, for a sense of even greater immediacy, some of the camera work was done from the back of a motorbike. Bursting onto the screen for what seemed like the first time was likeable young actress Carol White, playing Battersea girl Sylvie. In fact the diminutive Carol had already appeared as a juvenile in British film classics such as *The Belles of St Trinian's*, *Doctor in the House*, and *Carry On Teacher*, but had subsequently retired in disgust on becoming typecast in roles depicting what she called 'dull, very stupid blondes in skin-tight dresses and bouffant hairstyles' in terrible second-feature films. However, after giving birth to her two sons she had re-entered the business, finding roles in popular TV series such as *Emergency – Ward 10* and *Dixon of Dock Green*. She got the part in Ken Loach's play after a strong showing at her audition, when she was asked to improvise the part of a drunk wife coming out of the pub and being called a slut and a whore by her husband yelling from across the street. Her improvisation turned into a terrible fight, with Carol shouting out some dirty Cockney insults – thus clinching the deal for Ken. She was exactly the authentic type of actress that he was always to look for throughout his subsequent career. He found something quite touching in her performance, a warmth that came through the screen and made people want to watch her. But equally he felt there was a kind of sadness about Carol, sensing that she was never going to get where she wanted to be. For Tony Garnett, Carol's emotions were 'available to the character, the piece, the director and the camera. She was also vulnerable, and rather *too* vulnerable for her own good in life.'

Carol was impressive as Sylvie, very credible in the role and exuberantly singing *I Wanna Be Loved By You* in the pub – if throughout the play perhaps overdoing the whole fag-in-mouth bit. The character Fat Lil was played by actress Jessie Robins, later Ringo's auntie in *Magical Mystery Tour*. Just as full of life in the raw as Nell's original conception, the play made good use of Nell's talent for authentic dialogue and kept the same characters in much the same scenes: the girls in the sweet factory, the boys in the pub or on their motorbikes, the old woman in the factory complaining of getting 'the guitar' every winter from the damp and the repellent Tally Man disparaging his black clients.

For Tony Garnett, depicting Rube's abortion on screen, and as realistically as possible, was absolutely pivotal. His mother had died from a backstreet abortion when he was only five and alone in the house with her and his baby brother. As the police tried to track down her abortionist Tony's father committed suicide, and the two little boys were split up and sent to live with relatives. Tony's desperation to bring the horrors of abortion to public attention was behind the initial hoodwinking of management to get the project off the ground:

I told no one, not even Ken, that this scene alone would have persuaded me the film must be made. Ruby survives, but...I wanted no more unnecessary deaths or orphaned children. I hated the law and wanted it abolished. Those shocked by my ruthless deception at the BBC had no idea of its roots. I would have cut off my arm to get that scene in front of the public.

In a significant addition, a heartfelt protest not in the original novel was inserted. Before and after Rube's harrowing abortion scenes Ken and Tony used a voice-over from Tony's own GP on the effects of backstreet abortion:

In my surgery I see at least one woman a week who is seriously contemplating an abortion. Quite apart from the thirty-five deaths a year that we know are directly attributable to the backstreet abortions, the most common and seriously disturbing result must be that the girl is unable to have any more babies. She may be unable to have a family.

The foetus was not depicted.

The play, exposing as it did the prevalence, danger and horror of illegal operations, was transmitted at exactly the time a bill about abortion law reform was going through Parliament, and significantly contributed to the ever more urgent national debate around the subject. Abortion was legalised in 1967.

The televised *Up the Junction* (still available on YouTube) is lively and lyrical, teeming with noise and movement, its episodic nature giving viewers the impression they are right there with the characters out on the streets and in the pub. The spontaneity is deceiving, for the effects were cleverly calculated, and included the then fairly radical approach of using background pop music as a counterpoint to the action, much as Nell had done in the book: the Kinks' *I Need You* playing just after the husband and wife fight, and Ben E King's *Yes*, about a woman saying yes to a man, playing just after the abortion scene. The lyrics of the opening song *Bad Girl*, sung over shots of Clapham as the titles roll, were written by Nell herself.

Shot in black and white and in a grainy focus intentionally suggestive of documentary, *Up the Junction* was watched by nearly ten million people. Fifty viewers wrote in expressing approbation (including the vicar of St Marks in Battersea) but a record 464 viewers complained to the BBC about the bad language and depiction of sexual promiscuity, some labelling Nell 'depraved' and 'insane'; it was greeted with outrage from the *Daily Telegraph* and elsewhere. According to Tony Garnett all hell was let loose with headlines such as 'This must be just about THE LIMIT' in the *Daily Mail*, which also claimed that twenty GPs had sent a telegram to the British Medical Association requesting strong representations be made to the BBC to cease portraying moral laxity as normal.

The *Daily Mirror*, on the other hand, congratulated the BBC for having the honesty to show it and dubbed the play beautiful, moving, and funny. *Up the Junction* was '...raw and ruggedly honest...throbbed and bucked and stank with life...great tatty, lumpy, gristly, meaty hunks of everyday life'. It was a supreme relief to escape from the sort of sophistication in so many programmes that was merely a blind for falsity and dishonesty, the paper declared, and anybody who protested at the programme was protesting that people were people. However, the *Mirror* then rather spoiled its liberal stance by stating that the horrifying abortion scene must have done its bit to keep some girl viewers on the straight and narrow, and, despite its point about viewer protests, proceeded to print a rich selection of adverse comments from Battersea's older residents: 'disgusted', 'a slander', 'That programme has discredited all of us', 'Abortions and whoring in Battersea? That Miss Dunn wants knocking on the head'. Younger residents of the area, according to the *Mirror*, did admit the truth of the play, describing Clapham as a pretty sexy place.

Other reviews criticised the experimental nature of the shooting and the way the documentary style mixed fact and fiction ('viewers have a right to know whether what they are being offered is real or invented,' said one), although conceding that the technical innovations at least put the piece across with an impact which no conventional methods would likely have achieved. Ken responded that the use of documentary elements reflected the programme's scheduling: *The Wednesday Play* appeared immediately after the evening news, and he was keen for their plays 'not to be considered dramas but as continuations of the news'. Stern activist Mary Whitehouse, founder of the recent Clean Up TV Campaign, wrote to the Health Minister complaining as had the doctors that the BBC were promoting promiscuity as a normal thing, and that the denigration of womanhood was disastrous to national life. (Ken Loach was always proud that *Up the Junction* and his later TV play *Cathy Come Home* were amongst the first programmes Mary ever complained about.) She was later to write in her 1967 book *Cleaning Up TV* that the sooner terrible backstreet abortionists were put out of business the better, but suggested a play making clear that any kind of abortion, legal or otherwise, had dangers to mental and bodily health far greater than childbirth, and put forward her own alternative to unwanted pregnancy:

How about a programme which demonstrates that clean living could cut out a great deal of this problem at the root?

Nell had some reservations about Loach's version. A scene where the women working in the sweet factory all burst into song was a 'little bit pretty-pretty', while the doctor's voice-over she found heavy-handed and tending to distract from the drama. In retrospect she recognised this for what it was: 'It's a common enough fate of working-class characters in films, or indeed any kind of art: someone usually wants to draw a lesson from you.'

The BBC, meanwhile, had recognised both the excellence of the play and that all the publicity was good

145

for the ratings. The following year they announced a repeat but then backtracked after a wave of advance protest, BBC governors acknowledging the 'great offence' the piece caused on its first screening. However, they pointed to threats of an injunction – a Court order prohibiting or compelling a particular action, i.e. presumably that the play not be shown – as the reason for the cancellation. Controller of Programmes Huw Wheldon continued to insist that in his opinion it was the most outstanding and unignorable of all the Wednesday Plays, 'moral, vigorous, technically brand-new, accurate and fresh' (even though he had stipulated that a love-making scene be substantially cut in the repeat). The BBC was proud of it, he maintained, admiring both its technical brilliance and honesty of purpose, and had widely circulated all the positive press cuttings after its first airing.

When they did repeat *Up the Junction* in 1977 and again in 1993 much of the media finally acknowledged the play as the groundbreaker it really was, both in content and approach to filming – though not all the critics were won over. The *Daily Mail* continued its posturing with accusations that Nell Dunn had written out of a sense of middle-class guilt, and that the story had led to increased permissiveness, divorce and abortion in British life. For the *Observer* the stir the play had caused in the 1960s was understandable, with its documentary style and insistent presence of period pop songs, its 'novel portrayal of working-class culture, pubs, clubs, girls teasing their back-combed hair in the ladies', tea-breaks, greasy spoons, backstreet abortions', but now – it was boring. It had long since ceased to be a play to be enjoyed and was now merely a social document, the paper judged, recording a far distant time when people talked about being 'up the spout' or having 'a bit of the other' and when Battersea

Power Station actually was a power station. Only the truly great dramas of the last fifty years retained the power to entertain and to move, the review concluded, and *Up the Junction* was not amongst them.

As for Nell's Battersea friends, although perfectly happy when Nell had first read out her pieces to them, they were less so when the papers started writing that the play was disgraceful. 'They became very confused,' according to Nell. The girls took words like 'disgraceful' to refer to such things as the scene in the play where the boys and girls go swimming at night in Tooting Bec pool in their underwear (a cameraman had jumped into the pool alongside them to film the scene). Later in her life Nell would worry about the extent to which she had exploited them. She denied, however, that she in any way ran down the working class. 'If anything, I set out to expose the hardships of working-class life.'

Ken Loach went on to direct the devastating TV drama *Cathy Come Home*, the story of a homeless mother whose children are taken away from her. Carol White played the main role and her two young sons played the children, but this time the script was not from a work by Nell Dunn – coming, instead, from the pen of her writer husband Jeremy Sandford (described by Tony Garnett as dishevelled, his hair untamed by a comb, but 'oozing old Etonian charm and good manners, socially confident, seemingly oblivious to the impression he gave'). After moving across the river with Nell, Jeremy had been horrified to see people evicted and rendered homeless and put it all down on paper. Nell took the script to Tony, and public outcry following the resultant drama was a great boost to the coincidental opening of Shelter, the charity for the homeless.

After the appearance of *Up the Junction* on television, fledgling director Peter Collinson then produced a film version, with a soundtrack by songwriting duo Manfred Mann and Mike Hugg, which came out in 1968 – the first of the 'Angry Young Women' films not in moody black and white but glorious Technicolor. Ken Loach had not been interested in making it for the big screen. 'We felt we had done it as well as we could,' he commented.

The screenplay of the film departed substantially from the original novel with the introduction of new characters and storylines. Heiress Polly (Suzy Kendall) has come across the river from Chelsea and takes a job in a sweet factory where she befriends two working-class sisters, Sylvie and Rube, played by Maureen Lipman and Adrienne Posta. Jessie Robins again features, playing one of the factory workers. Polly finds a dingy flat to live in and starts going out with the boy who delivers some second-hand furniture for her, Peter, played by a young Dennis Waterman.

She cuts her hair, adopts the Battersea fashion of lurid minidress and dangly earrings and starts to feel a part of it all: 'It's more real, more natural,' she says of her new environment. 'You're free to be yourself.' But Peter can't understand her: he hates Battersea, envies Polly's access to an easy existence and is frustrated by her rejection of the moneyed lifestyle. When Sylvie is involved in a street brawl with her estranged husband, and Rube becomes pregnant and has a traumatic illegal abortion, he tries to convince Polly that life in Battersea is squalid and frustrating. Tragedy then strikes when Rube's boyfriend Terry is killed in a motorcycle accident. Polly agrees to go with Peter for a weekend by the sea; he picks her up in an E-Type Jaguar, which he says he has hired, and insists on staying in the best hotel. There is a quarrel which shows up their differing points of view about life and Peter leaves in anger; Polly next sees him in court charged with stealing the sports car. After he has been sentenced they meet briefly in his police cell, still very far apart from understanding each other as the film ends.

Nell did not write the screenplay but according to Peter Collinson provided a deal of material not contained in the book. Dennis Waterman thought that the writing had been softened from Nell's original, probably as a result of the film's American backing. He suggested that it should be in black and white to harden things up and get a more realistic feel, but this was deemed likely to have a detrimental effect on sales. They were aiming for a 'big, brash, colourful, swinging London' effect, Dennis realised – which he felt was not quite the spirit of the original.

Dennis' father was a ticket collector at Clapham Junction and Peter Collinson viewed the young man as a solidly working-class actor right for the part, although instructing Dennis to have his hair lightened and cut more trendily for the role. Peter would take him and former top model Suzy out for lunches in his 'Roller', making nineteen-year-old Dennis feel like a real film star. For Dennis it was exciting and romantic and he promptly fell for the leading lady – in his words the most attractive woman he had ever met. 'She was exquisite...astonishingly nice.' Both had existing partners, in Suzy's case her future husband Dudley Moore, but Dennis' feelings were reciprocated and the lovers sometimes risked meeting in the flat she and Dudley shared. According to Dennis they never 'misbehaved' there, luckily so as Dudley one day surprised Dennis playing his piano, but seemingly without suspecting anything. The affair eventually folded, Dennis admitting he had been out of his depth.

At the glittering *Up the Junction* premiere – to Dennis' disappointment, held at his local cinema, the Granada at Clapham Junction – he was 'gobsmacked' to see on screen the massive letters spelling out his and Suzy's names as the leads. 'I'm a star! I'm a star!' The film's publicists had run competitions and promotions in the local papers so that the real residents from 'up the Junction' would have the first chance to see the film, and a sizeable contingent of local youths were in the audience. At the end of what was intended to be a romantic, sensitive scene between the on-screen lovers there was a big close-up of Dennis saying 'Do me a favour, seduce me.' The line was greeted with howls of 'You wanker!'

The poster for the film, rated X, hinted at the content: 'Don't get caught was what she wasn't taught'. The word 'bugger' – in previous films a big problem for the British Board of Film Censors – was this time allowed because, in the words of the increasingly lenient board, it was 'a part of the natural speech of the kind of people shown in this semi-documentary'. Similarly, a successful, if disturbing, backstreet abortion was permitted to be shown, whereas in times gone by the Board had anguished over any possible offence or suggestion that abortion was a valid solution to unwanted pregnancy.

Unlike Ken's TV play the film – not very credible and really only a pale imitation of the TV production – did not have much impact or cause much controversy. The British Film Institute's *Monthly Film Bulletin* noted that the stronger storyline gave greater cohesion to Nell Dunn's rather disjointed collection of episodes in that Polly's relationship with Peter acted as a thread drawing it all together. Polly's naïve attitude that working-class people were somehow more real was matched by Peter's juvenile belief that money and fast cars were the key to happiness, the review observed, and the brief idyll between the two misguided young people was sensitively handled by the director. Not so the scenes in Battersea. Factory life, the drunken brawl in the street, a rowdy sing-song in a pub all emerged as caricature, the *Bulletin* complained, mostly because shooting such scenes close-up in Technicolor produced an effect of huge exaggeration and demonstrated the inexperience of the makers of the film. For the *Kensington Post* the film was spoiled by its 'disquieting fascination with the proletariat'. The *Times* complained that the little vignettes of working-class life were filmed in a 'relentlessly emphatic manner, all giant close-ups and art angles', while the plot about the rich girl coming over the river and getting involved with a Battersea boy was rather silly, with Suzy Kendall unconvincing because her accent was the same as everyone else's (not the case, in fact, as the character speaks with noticeable poshness). The film was self-conscious and condescending in its picture of working-class life, the reviewer finished, and while Dickens might have recognised the characters the present-day inhabitants of Battersea would merely find them quaint.

Across the Atlantic *Playboy USA* was all for it: 'wealthy bird' Polly, a ninny for whom slums were a choice, not a birthright, was fetchingly played by Suzy, and director Peter Collinson never patronised working-class characters like the 'magnificently common tarts' played by Maureen Lipman and Adrienne Posta. Flavourful and unsentimental, was the verdict. For *Maclean's* magazine in Canada only an excellent supporting cast gave the film more than 'ho-hum interest'.

Nell was reportedly less than thrilled with the film version, upset that her original shadowy narrator had morphed into a distinct character very much based on herself who had been made the focus of the action, instead of the Battersea women who were her real subject.

§

Meanwhile, Nell continued to write. Her next work was *Talking to Women* in 1965, a transcription of nine conversations she had taped with young women in their mid to late twenties – a radical idea at the time (and one she would repeat many years later with older women on the subject of being a grandmother). The group was clearly intended as a spectrum across the classes, with one of the women working in a factory, although in fact they were mainly middle-class creative types and included writer Edna O'Brien. The theme of the book is the shifting lives of women in that era and whether life could change for the better; Nell described the work as a feminist project 'because it's about women, and about women counting, and about women being interesting'. She asked each of the interviewees about politics, economic survival, domesticity, life lived with or without children, and whether marriage was out of date. She wanted to know the meaning of passion and whether passion was just sex, and if they thought sex was important; and about hope, love, class, creativity, and what the women thought the future would bring them. Nell's deep conviction that women's lives should be worth more is reflected in her preface:

If these girls have anything in common it is a belief in personal fulfilment – that a woman's life should not solely be the struggle to make men happy but more than that a progress towards the development of one's own body and soul...

Talking to Women, Nell Dunn, 1965

A goal that needed to be fought for, as she makes clear in the book. 'Shouldn't one be out fighting for freedom?'

Photograph: Tina Tranter

Then came her possibly most famous work. One day in Battersea Nell had come across a young woman with golden hair standing outside her house, her thin white legs in slippers. They got to know each other and Nell's new acquaintance – referred to by Nell as Josie – began to demonstrate how to live for the moment, encouraging her to climb on the back of a strange boy's motorbike or to pursue other adventures (including introducing her to a beautiful Soho prostitute who worked in a grand way, with a maid and dresser). Nell wanted to get down what it was like being young and female in a poor environment, with no money and no career. The 'freedom and daring' of Josie's way of living, her attempts to get the most out of a hard life, made a deep impression on Nell, and she made her friend the central character of a novel. Because *Up the Junction* had by now sold over 500,000 copies, she was able to command £10,000 for the paperback rights to the new work, *Poor Cow*, published in 1967.

The poor cow of the title, skinny young Joy with her bare, 'slum-white legs' and bleached hair, is left alone with her beloved baby boy Jonny when husband Tom is sent to prison for robbery. They go to live in a single room with raddled Auntie Emm, Joy dreaming of having a car and a place of her own with fitted carpets. Before long she starts an affair with Tom's friend Dave, finding herself sexually awakened and truly in love for the first time. They move into a flat and she and Jonny and Dave experience real happiness – for Joy, even going to the launderette with Dave is a laugh. Then Dave gets a twelve-year stretch for robbery with violence. Joy is left disconsolate as she moves back in with Emm, but does not sit around feeling sorry for herself: she finds enjoyable work as a barmaid and as a nude model, though slipping into promiscuity and semi-prostitution. After serving two years her husband Tom gets out of prison and they try again, living in a depressing flat in Catford. Tom becomes ever more violent and controlling as Joy thinks longingly about having a baby girl to make her happy again. The final chapter, Desolation, ends on a note of hope and humour. Jonny gets lost when Tom is supposed to be looking after him; Joy searches desperately, terrified, but finally discovers the little boy in an abandoned house. She realises the only thing that really matters is that her son should be all right and that they should be together, and they head for home:

'Oh gawd, what a state I'm in,' she said, as, hand in hand, they walked back down the deserted road. 'To think when I was a kid I planned to conquer the world and if anyone saw me now they'd say, 'She's had a rough night, poor cow.'

Poor Cow, Nell Dunn, 1967

The voice of the novel alternates between Joy's inner musings and a third-person narrative which allows the reader a more objective view. It's uneven, with perhaps rather too many ill-spelt love letters to Dave in prison and long screeds of unpunctuated streams of consciousness from Joy, but like *Up the Junction* the work positively bursts with life: Joy walking down the road in the sunshine, Joy enjoying sleeping with any man she fancies and showing off her body as a nude model, Auntie Emm and Joy's barmaid friend Beryl raucously recounting their unfettered love lives in long dialogues delivered in a rich cockney. Snatches of Sixties songs from the transistor playing Radio London at full blast are the soundscape to Joy's experiences (*You've Got To Hide Your Love Away* by the Beatles, *Stand By Me* by Ben E King, *Monday Monday* by the Mamas & the Papas); her dreams and wants are shaped by women's magazines and brand names – Prestige Happymaid, Pepsi – which also serve to point up the contrast with reality. 'Fuck that,' Joys says, looking at a Pepsi poster of golden girls frolicking on a beach while she eats cottage pie in a café, her newborn son laid on the scratched bench beside her. The setting is again vibrant South London, buzzing with cosy pubs and greasy cafés and High Street sales – dingy, littered, and occasionally glorious.

Joy and the other women in the novel seem free to live their lives as they please, to work where they want and to love as they want without heed to morals or middle-class respectability. They talk frankly and cheerfully and prey on men, casually offering sexual services for money; the women talk about going 'up West', a euphemism for prostitution (Joy refuses to go, although she is willing to have sex with a driving instructor to get her certificate). Female sexual pleasure is taken for granted – a mostly new departure in novel writing. Until *Poor Cow,* the treatment of women's sexuality in novels was often either discreet or non-existent, but here almost for the first time is a frank admission of sexual feeling: Joy's pleasure in seeing the faint dust on the bare backs of men on building sites, the different behaviours she notes between her various partners and her reflections on what constitutes a good lover:

Proper lusty I was getting – it used to be love but it's all lust now – it's so terrific with different blokes. Sometimes you fancy it all soft and other times you want them to fuck the life out of you. Well you can't get that from the same bloke can you.

Poor Cow, Nell Dunn, 1967

Not unconnectedly, Nell also beautifully conveys the pleasure Joy takes in the sensual feel and smell of her child. The absolute love that she has for her son makes itself felt in the frequent passages describing Jonny's clothes or toys – his little trousers and Wellington boots, the way he passes his toy tractor from one hand to the other as Joy pulls his jumper over his head. She also begins to long for another child, a girl this time to spoil and dress up. As in the descriptions of female sexuality, this evocation of deep maternal feeling was a fairly new phenomenon. Paired with Joy's promiscuity and nude modelling her excellent, affectionate mothering might make for an uneasy mix for some, but renders Joy a far more complex character than the traditional, mutually exclusive alternatives of tart or mother.

But Nell's characters were not as free as they appeared. Dig deeper into the narrative and it can be seen that women's lives were still constrained by male control of finances and by male violence – and, inevitably, by biology, despite the dawning of the age of the pill. *Poor Cow* includes yet another abortion, Joy graphically describing how she helps a friend through the ordeal and how the husband disposes of the foetus. And Joy's future ultimately holds nothing but subservience to her husband and the life of a housewife, all that is really available to her. Throughout the novel Joy has longed for security, but once back with her husband on his return from prison she is soon bored and frustrated with domestic life and the claustrophobia of the female world:

How can I go back to all this – I'm not the same any more. I can't stick this sort of security. I can't stick all these women and their kids. I love kids, I'd break the world in half for my Jonny but it's being bogged down every blessed moment and all day among women. You go in the shops, it's bleeding women – you go in the park, it's bleeding women...I just want to be something – I can't be nothing all my life...

Poor Cow, Nell Dunn, 1967

Reactions to the novel were a mixed bag. The *Times Literary Supplement* talked of Nell Dunn working hard to 'introduce us to those lower-class citizens whom we so rarely know as neighbours' (excusing itself as using the term 'lower-class' simply as a statement of fact, and not meant patronisingly). Its critic was surprised about the unsentimental way Nell treated her characters as equals: her passive approach suggested that there was 'something to be respected, almost envied, in the warm, dodgy, half-criminal life' lived by Joy, despite her troubles. This was a serious and moving little book, concluded the review, although scarcely a novel. The *Times* was more blistering, referring to Joy's 'interminable, and embarrassing' letters to Dave in prison and deeming the book all very authentic – in the way a tape-recorder is authentic. Realism was obviously at a premium in *Poor Cow*, said the paper, but the book was totally unrealistic in that none of the characters came alive, there was no sense of their lives being felt from the inside, and in short no sign that Miss Dunn could write anything that came near to being a novel. 'Nell Dunn's reportage is as good as ever,' remarked a frosty Claire Tomalin in the *Observer*. The novel was curiously voyeuristic, weighed in the *Spectator*, not only as regards Joy's 'sexual ruminations' as might be expected, but also in its intense focus on the social and class minutiae of Joy's world. Author John Braine, of the 'Angry Young Man' brigade, declared 'I was disgusted, I was nauseated, I was saddened – but I wasn't bored'.

A 'very severe man' asked Nell on live television whether she didn't think it irresponsible to promote promiscuity. Her comeback, to his surprise, was to state that in a way she believed in promiscuity because it was simply looking for somebody to fall permanently in love with: women needed to try different men. 'I was quite proud of that because at the time it was quite subversive.' She certainly did not feel that what she had written was wrong, and in subsequent years found it 'terribly funny' that this had been suggested. In those days there was a lot of cruelty and hypocrisy about, she observed.

With her latest work in the news Nell was unexpectedly invited to address prisoners at Maidstone Jail, where she chose to read them the sections from *Poor Cow* about prison life. The reaction was enthusiastic, so much so that the prison authorities asked her to stop reading, but the men booed and roared and she decided to keep on. They were a very positive audience, Nell reported (adding that she often visited friends in prison and was fascinated by it).

Inevitably, with the passage of time, *Poor Cow* now seems less startling. Much of its innovation has been reproduced elsewhere. To modern tastes Joy might seem obsessed with sex and over-dependent on the love of men for her happiness; her willingness to exhibit herself to men is unattractive. She dislikes the company of other women. But *Poor Cow* still retains the power to shock, particularly the description of abortion, and Joy herself remains just that, a joy: perceptive, melancholy and deeply dissatisfied with her lot, but always exuberantly alive.

§

Nell wanted *Poor Cow* to be made into a film and Ken Loach found himself back on the job, this time directing his first cinema feature from a screenplay that he co-authored with Nell (now living in Putney). Ken, who lived in nearby Barnes, would walk over to Nell's to ask for more dialogue for a particular scene and Nell would duly supply it – although according to the film's actor Terence Stamp much of it was unscripted and, in an effort to achieve spontaneity, the actors were sometimes given completely different directions for the same scene.

Carol White, whom both Ken and Nell had envisaged as Joy from the start, took the central role opposite Terence Stamp's gentle portrayal of Dave (privately, according to Carol, the two enjoyed a 'brief but consuming affair'). Ken had wanted an unknown but was obliged to accept the already famous Terence, who Ken acknowledged was always very pleasant and worked very hard, but gave *Poor Cow* more the aura of a film than the grainier product he had in mind. Terry's agent insisted he have a caravan on set, despite Ken having stipulated no trailers or special treatment to Carol, who of course immediately wanted a caravan too. The whole thing escalated, remembered Ken, although he was sure that if Terry had been approached properly by the film's producer there would not have been a problem.

The plot remained much the same as in the book. As before, Loach shot in the streets of London and elsewhere, and involved real people in the action. Three of the background songs came from pop star Donovan, his gentle, plangent strains another instance of music being used to provide a striking contrast to the grit of the story and point up the differences between romance and reality. The style of the film was Loach's trademark semi-documentary, a series of scenes from Joy's life, if departing to some extent from his predilection for handheld camera. His intention in the film was to show the 'colossal waste', Joy's huge appetite for living despoiled by her hopeless environment.

Carol White was from working-class roots herself and was all too aware of the honesty and reality of Nell's storyline:

We wanted to show what can happen to a girl in the slums. These people really exist. They don't ask for much in life, but their own lack of knowledge about life and their own ignorance about how to get a job and get out of their environment does them in. Even if you're pretty, your accent loses you the job, and you fall back on the easy way out – stealing, or nude modelling, or hitting the streets. I could've ended up like that.

In the scene where her character Joy does nude modelling for a group of seedy so-called amateur photographers, Carol was initially embarrassed and insistent that she keep something on, then became so involved she peeled everything off and 'actually enjoyed it'. The actors playing the photographers were meant not to have any film in their cameras, but Carol heard film whirring and Ken stopped the shoot to investigate. A man was discovered taking shots for real and thrown off the set.

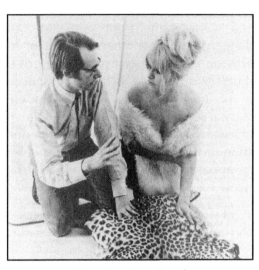

Ken directing Carol

Opening with what was considered to be a shocking sequence of Joy giving birth to her son Jonny, the film (in colour) begins with Joy and Tom and new baby Jonny settled in a bright, modern flat with a television, a humorous intertitle (an item of printed text inserted between the filmed action) first telling us that 'The world was our oyster...and we chose Ruislip.' The voice of the intertitle is Joy's: the action is virtually always seen from her perspective, with the intermittent interior monologue of the novel transferred to a voice-over. After Tom goes to prison and Joy moves to stay with her aunt, we see her boiling her son's nappies in a large pan and living in a grim environment of damp walls and peeling paper.

As in the novel, she eventually moves into a similarly rundown flat with Dave and they enjoy their time together as a makeshift family, all three going on a trip to Wales where a waterfall and a drawling trumpet soundtrack provide a romantic backdrop to a lingering kiss between the lovers.

After Dave's sentencing for robbery Joy gets the job as a barmaid, wearing her hair up and dressing in a low-cut, tight-fitting dress as she flirts with customers; in the photo shoot scene – which appears deliberately titillating – she and her friend Beryl, played by Kate Williams, pose in fluffy negligees and then in less and less clothing.

Still closely following the original storyline, Joy misses Dave and visits him in prison, where he confronts her with stories he has heard of her promiscuity. When husband Tom is finally released from his own sentence Joy goes back to him. One evening, after being slapped about by Tom, she goes out and returns to find Tom in front of the TV and Jonny missing. After a believably frantic search she finds the little boy alone on a demolition site where he has gone to play. Realising how much Jonny means to her, she decides to stay with her husband despite the abuse, but continues to dream of a future with Dave. In the very last scene – again, calling to mind a documentary – Joy is facing camera as she talks to an unseen interviewer on a number of subjects introduced by intertitles: The Future, My Perfect Life, and Thinking of Dave. The camera lingers on her face in a freeze-frame as the film concludes.

The British Board of Film Censors demanded cuts to certain sexual references but still rated the film as an X. It was a surprise success at the box office, selling to the US for more than its production cost and doing extremely well, especially in Italy, perhaps because of the popularity there of realist filmmaking. The *Daily Mirror* liked its gusto and raw vitality, and praised Ken's astute, compassionate eye. Film critic Dilys Powell in the *Sunday Times* enthused that it was 'often very funny, often bawdy, always miraculously fluent, as apparently spontaneous as if lived, not acted'.

The *Times*, on the other hand, commented that this 'picturesque tale of casual and drifting prostitution...decked out with snippets of *cinéma-vérité* interview, printed captions and such-like' was a copy of more original French and American directing work and demonstrated the derivative nature of Ken Loach's style. Style apart, the *Times* continued, the content of *Poor Cow* – its view of the 'raw vitality, sexual potency, and tangy outspokenness of the working classes' – had a maddeningly patronising air, the characters made coarse and wayward by their bourgeois creators. Even the love-making had more in common with the sort of arty film the characters would never have seen than with the realities of working-class life, the critic sniffed. The film equated the working classes with the criminal classes, none of the characters emerged as credible individuals, and the improvisatory nature of much of the dialogue only served to remind that these were actors acting (specifically singling out Terence Stamp). Carol White, too, came in for criticism for looking too like actress Julie Christie – hardly her fault – and was accused of cultivating the resemblance.

Verging on sentimentality, said the British Film Institute's *Monthly Film Bulletin,* an incongruous mixture of realism and romanticism and a superficial, slightly patronising incursion into the nether realms. The Institute's other publication *Sight and Sound*, however, liked the performances Ken had elicited from the cast, particularly the marvellously warm and likeable portrait from Carol White as Joy – even if decrying the mix of styles, the wild ranging of atmosphere from the love scenes in Wales to the almost music-hall comedy of the 'modelling' for the dirty mac brigade. (*Sight and Sound*, to its credit, also predicted that Ken Loach would go on to make better and more important films.)

There were further acid comments. A female critic in the *Sunday Telegraph* complained that the opening birth scene was in bad taste, all the more so because it was in colour.

'Like all births, except those with which you're personally concerned, it's a messy sight. It isn't dramatic, or informative, or vital to the story and no woman I know, whether she's had children of her own or not, particularly wants to watch the process.' Another reviewer likened the scene in which Joy and Dave kiss in front of a Welsh waterfall to a cigarette advert, while the *Illustrated London News* asked why anyone would take any sort of pleasure in watching such feckless, worthless, mindless and unprincipled people: Joy and Dave as characters were 'fundamentally boring'.

Nell herself was satisfied with the way the film turned out: 'I was happy and I absolutely loved the character of Joy.' She liked Carol's acting, finding something 'very delicate and lovely about her'. She was especially pleased that Ken had included in the film what she considered the most subversive element in *Poor Cow*, Joy's stated enjoyment of different men's bodies. 'I always liked that...it shocked everybody!' Ken, though, was not so happy. He had liked Nell's book and believed the film did not really live up to it, mainly because he was 'somewhat overwhelmed' by making his first cinema feature. He thought he made a very bad job of it – that he had not been sufficiently self-critical, or well organised – and confessed to not knowing enough about the film-making process to find his way through the jungle of a large feature unit. But it was a salutary experience, he acknowledged, in that he gained some idea of how unnecessary a lot of the circus of feature film work actually was. Looking back from the present century Ken felt he had achieved a taste of the times, at least; the film had many little ideas in it that worked quite well, and Carol's character came across reasonably well. On the other hand, he suspected that if he saw it again he might find some of *Poor Cow* 'absolutely indescribable'.

It was a good book. The problem was that I just made a bad film. I framed the shots badly, timed them badly, cut them badly. It's the equivalent of bad prose. I just wasn't good enough, and I suppose that it was partly because it was my first film, but also because the story hadn't the same drive as Cathy, and Junction, I didn't think through the content sufficiently. It was a mess, and it was my fault.

Terence Stamp went on to enjoy a long acting career, and many years later scenes from *Poor Cow* were included in his film *The Limey*, as supposed flashbacks to the early life of the criminal character he was playing. Carol White's was a less fortunate story. Ken Loach viewed her as exploited and ripped off, very vulnerable to flattery and being told she was going to be the next big star. In his opinion she was already losing her grip during the *Poor Cow* filming, having received too much attention for her roles in *Up the Junction* and *Cathy Come Home*. She was being offered other parts, and Ken unwisely agreed to let her act in another film at the same time because Carol wanted to appear prettier on screen than she felt she was coming across as the downtrodden Joy. Ken was telling her to go home on the Tube while the other unit were collecting her in a big car – in his view, treating her with 'all that stupid flattery and nonsense that destroys people'.

Dubbed the Battersea Bardot by the press, beautiful, exuberant Carol eventually tried to make it in Hollywood, where she was (inevitably) hailed as the new Julie Christie. There was fleeting success but real stardom proved elusive. Drink and drugs followed and she returned to Britain, where she was given the sack by the managers of Nell Dunn's later stage play *Steaming*, reportedly for missing fifteen performances when on drugs. Nell felt Carol's performance was 'absolutely wonderful' but that she couldn't handle being in the play; her departure was greatly to Nell's sadness. Carol died in the US in 1991 while still only in her forties. The cause of death has been disputed, with some sources suggesting liver damage, others a drug overdose. A television film of her life, *The Battersea Bardot*, appeared in 1994.

§

According to her own account Nell's few years in Battersea had come to an end when the sanitary inspector found silverfish, a scaly insect, under the lino in her house and declared the home unfit for human habitation. Along with many other old dwellings in the area her terrace was eventually demolished and concrete skyscrapers erected in their place. A whole way of life was demolished at the same time, a network of friends and family that could never be reconstituted in the bleak tower blocks into which people were shunted.

Nell was extremely famous after *Up the Junction* and *Poor Cow* but felt rather bruised by her notoriety. There was an 'unhappy time', she admitted. She retreated to country life. A parting from husband Jeremy Sandford came in 1971, though they did not divorce for another eight years.

Living in Exmoor with her three children Nell grew bored with having no artistic life and no one to talk to, and returned to London. She joined a long-running therapist-led women's group and by 2017 had clocked up thirty-five years as a member. 'There's only six women in it, and so we just explore what's happening in each of our lives, really, in what feels like a very safe place with a confidentiality clause,' Nell explained. This abiding interest in women's experience continued to be reflected in her writing: in 1981 she made a splash with her comedy play *Steaming*, about the reaction of six very different women to the threatened closure of their local Turkish baths (first staged at London's Theatre Royal, Stratford, scene of Shelagh Delaney's triumph with *A Taste of Honey*). Nell wrote the play after starting to go to the steam baths in Hackney and becoming extremely interested in the way women spoke to each other when alone. The script initially just reflected her usual desire to capture what was happening around her, but turned more political when the baths became scheduled to close and finally did so. The loss of the baths greatly upset the women who used them because it was their special place, although there was no campaigning against the closure as with Nell's characters. (On completing *Steaming* Nell simply took the script to the stage door of the Duke of York's Theatre in London and asked them to give it to the director, who agreed to put it on. It was later made into an underwhelming film starring Vanessa Redgrave, Sarah Miles, Diana Dors and Brenda Bruce.)

She went on to write further works for the stage, including *Cancer Tales* in 2003, a series of five linked, short plays telling the story of seven women who were either cancer patients themselves or their close relatives. Each told the story of one cancer journey, all of them true accounts taken down verbatim from conversations with patients, carers and medical staff, Nell's art being in the careful selection and editing. The play was inspired by Nell's experience in her forties of the death from cancer of her father, which she had found difficult to handle – not knowing how to help him or cope with it herself, and subsequently living in denial for many years. Her stated aim in writing the play a quarter of a century later was to get 'more friendly with death', to let it become part of ordinary life.

When her partner of thirty-five years, the American computer mathematician Dan Oestreicher, was later diagnosed with lung cancer and sent home to die, Nell was able to make his remaining months happy ones. They had always spent every night together but had lived separately so that Nell could have an empty place to write in and Dan his own space; now, he moved across the road into Nell's. She stopped writing to care for him, and they lay next to each other on the bed in the afternoons talking and laughing, receiving visits from friends and family. But on the day Dan died in 2009, when Nell was in her early seventies, there was what she called a 'series of blunders' attending his death which made her very angry, and she became a patron of Dignity in Dying, the campaign to improve end-of-life decisions.

§

Rereading *Up the Junction* and *Poor Cow* in the twenty-first century, Nell could remember her excitement during that period in Battersea when she was young enough to believe that she was immortal and the thrills of life were never going to end,

...when the day began around six, eating fresh rolls on the way to work, and often ended after midnight kissing somewhere forbidden, someone forbidden.

Up the Junction caused such a sensation because of the backstreet abortion element, believed Nell (who could remember visiting a family planning clinic in 1959 where unmarried women were not permitted to use the service). She was very surprised when the book came out that people were so shocked by it, and was always to recall writer John Braine's comment that the stories were disgusting and nauseating. She did not think the success of *Up the Junction* changed her that much, coming as it did only after her long apprenticeship learning to write and seven years of constant rejection from publishers. After its appearance she simply went on writing, still ambitious to achieve: the 'Angry Young Men' had been producing for a while but not that many women, she recalled. But fifty years later Nell was clear that it was life that mattered to her, not writing.

As for *Poor Cow,* Nell continued over the years to defend Joy against the accusations of promiscuity, maintaining as she did at the time that it was more a search for love and the right person, and that it didn't really matter when Joy changed from man to man because she truly loved each one. Joy saying she wanted different men's bodies was 'wonderfully outrageous' and Nell loved her: 'There was something very free about her.' The character was partly herself as a young mother and partly the real Joy, Nell admitted. She insisted that none of her characters had been totally based on anyone who might have recognised themselves when the book was published – although conceding that any such recognition likely did not happen because perhaps the crucial people (those in Battersea) never read it.

She returned to Joy's story in *My Silver Shoes*, published in 1996. It is twenty years later and Joy has left her violent husband Tom. She is holding down a good job where she can be proud of herself, but gradually things go wrong: her grown son Jonny deserts from the Army, her new partner leaves her. Joy's life dwindles to caring for her increasingly demented mother, whom she continues to love and will never abandon. But her vitality and likeability remain, London itself is as vibrant as ever, and the ending is upbeat. Joy will survive.

§

Some twenty years after the publication of Nell Dunn's two most famous works, new editions were published in the Virago Modern Classics series. In the introduction to *Up the Junction*, Mersey poet Adrian Henri wrote that for him Nell's early writing had permanent meaning. He commented that when he first read the book it was 'eminently readable, not to say un-put-downable', written almost as poetry and chiming with the new realism of the era. Reading it again so many years later, it remained just as readable and relevant, surprisingly so in that Nell's work encompassed much that was ephemeral: Top 20 hits, the price of shoes, adverts in shop windows. The answer for Adrian was that Nell's writing presented a poetic distillation of place and time that went beyond story, and that the subject was as much Nell herself – her perceptions, her non-judgement, her lack of condescension – as the people she described, and therefore still of significance. It had taken a Chelsea heiress to articulate the hopes, desires and delusions of working-class women, Adrian observed. The women were still real across the years, 'boozing, loving, laughing, crying...they live on'. He believed that Nell could be seen as a feminist, or perhaps a pre-feminist. In these two books, and in her subsequent works, the reader was aware of women as people, talking honestly and directly – part of the scandal that greeted her work was the sense almost of eavesdropping on women talking about sex as uninhibitedly as men, he felt. Her later output would more explicitly embrace the political dimension – particularly her stage play *Steaming* – but for Adrian the elements of feminism in the first two books are there, extractable rather than concretely present.

In the introduction to the new edition of *Poor Cow*, meanwhile, Nell's friend Margaret Drabble wrote how Nell in Battersea had found friendship, community, and warmth, instead of the respectability and reserve of her own kind:

The openness, the quick responses, the lawlessness of the women she met there struck her as something new, invigorating, liberating...a world where women did not depend on male patronage, where they went their own ways, sexually and financially, where there was plenty of work, so much work that they could afford to be cheeky, rebellious, loud-mouthed.

She observed that Nell had been excited by the humour and the energy, the violence and the freedom, and it had seemed a real world where women could lead real lives. To Nell the women had not seemed oppressed, despite their low pay. There was a sense of matriarchy; women were openly strong, rather than 'deviously influential.' After writing her books Nell had been hailed as akin to the 'Angry Young Men', Margaret Drabble recalled, a female writing of the lives of working-class women in a way that struck the same chords as the plays and novels of John Osborne and John Braine. For Margaret, Nell's reports of life in South London were 'simple, apparently artless, sympathetic, participatory' and, as she declared elsewhere, 'beautifully, lyrically written'. Nell had succeeded in the difficult task of writing across the class divide without sentimentality or condescension, never hitting a wrong note, her characters existing freely, in their own world. *Poor Cow* was 'touching, truthful and fresh...written with an unselfconscious elegance that conceals its craft'.

Did Nell herself believe she had been a feminist all those years ago? 'I definitely was,' she confirmed, stating that she had taken both Germaine Greer's *The Female Eunuch* and Simone de Beauvoir's *The Second Sex* very seriously. But she had never set out to break taboos or influence politicians, she stressed; in fact it would never have occurred to her that politicians would read anything she wrote. As far as she was concerned there was no feminist agenda in her writing, and in any case Nell was always clear that women needed and loved men. As she later commented about her play *Steaming*, 'I'm not sure if that comes into the feminist code.'

§

And what of Josie, the young woman Nell had befriended in Battersea who was the model for her fictional character Joy? There was a series of ever more disreputable men, including an inept criminal who got into trouble with the law trying to steal things for her, and a sugar daddy who turned out to be not as rich as she might have liked. But still Josie enjoyed life, her philosophy always to get the most out of it and let tomorrow take care of itself. She and Nell never lost touch, seeing and writing to each other for decades. They had an incredibly close relationship, observed the writer:

And people can't quite understand it, you know, because she's totally working class. Every now and again she says, "I wish I'd had a proper education". Her spelling is worse than mine and mine is very bad. But I don't think she particularly feels sorry for herself. She's had an exciting life, and a full life. She's worked all her life – often cleaning. But she has her life, nobody has told her what to do. I think this feels very important to her. And to me. I wasn't told what to do either.

For Nell she was an inspiration, the relationship between them intensely connected with her work as a writer. Josie's language and the way she lived her life were at the heart of *Poor Cow*, *My Silver Shoes*, and *Steaming*, said Nell, and in 2020 she published the story of their deep friendship – *The Muse, A memoir of love at first sight*.

She did the living. I did the writing.

The Millstone

Margaret Drabble

*When...I found that I was pregnant...I was obliged once more
to fall back on the dimly reported experiences of friends and
information I had gleaned through the years from cheap
fiction...It took me some time to summon up the courage: I sat
for a whole day in the British Museum, damp with fear...and
thinking about gin. I knew vaguely about gin, that it was
supposed to do something or other to the womb, quinine or
something I believe, and that combined with a hot bath it
sometimes works, so I decided that other girls had gone
through with it, so why not me. One might be lucky. I had no
idea how much gin one was supposed to consume, but I had a
nasty feeling that it was a whole bottle: the prospect of this
upset me both physically and financially. I grudged the
thought of two pounds on a bottle of gin, just to make myself
ill.*

   The Millstone, Margaret Drabble, 1965

§

Margaret Drabble was born in Sheffield in 1939, the
second of three daughters, her father a barrister who was
later a Labour candidate in two elections and who
ultimately became a judge. He and Margaret's mother
were the first in their families to go to university; the
house was always full of books, and they encouraged their
three girls and one son to read widely and to aim for
academic success. But things were difficult at home: both
parents were depressives. For Margaret's mother Kathleen
domesticity was boring and disappointing and she was
deeply dissatisfied; she often used to say she could have
been a writer, but never wrote anything, and to her fury it
was Margaret's father who produced two novels. Kathleen
had had to choose between a teaching career and
marriage, and despite her choice being marriage, behaved
with great anger and bitterness towards her husband. She

178

felt that life had not granted her what she deserved, although in Margaret's later opinion she in fact had everything: a caring husband, a comfortable home, three dutiful daughters and a son to be proud of. It was as though nothing was ever quite enough, and when she saw other doors opening for her daughters Kathleen wanted to go through them herself when it was too late. She was an 'unpredictable, unhappy and often terrifying person,' said Margaret, one whose 'angry depression...clearly related to her inertia and frustration, which afflicted so many educated and half-educated women of her generation'. Kathleen dominated and manipulated her children and they lived in terror of her rages and unpredictable moods, as did their mostly silent father John, a tender, gentle man who would try to comfort them all if distressed. Kathleen was particularly demanding of Margaret, her favourite, who was 'expected to be brilliant'; their relationship was tormented.

Margaret's relationship with her older sister Sue, meanwhile, was 'uncomfortable', at root a battle for their father's affection. Sue – who became the novelist Antonia Byatt – had known their father before he left to serve in the war, and on his return was forced to share him with her upstart sibling. Antonia was also despatched to a grandmother when very ill as a child, and the adult Margaret felt she must have suffered a Freudian anxiety on being sent away while her younger sister remained at home with their parents. With these difficulties between the two, and with their mother favouring Margaret, the atmosphere in the house could be fraught. Kathleen had a 'really foul temper' and was always telling Margaret off. She never told her daughters they looked pretty, or were nicely dressed; it was always all about their academic success. While still a child Margaret began to suffer from occasional deep depression herself – even having her hair drop out during one intense episode – and to stammer from anxiety. She took to reading the kind of tragic dramas and novelists, like Thomas Hardy, that told her existence wasn't all fun, and thought it wonderful to have a writer telling her that things were 'really, really awful'. She worried that she was going to go to hell, and thought she had done something terribly wrong without knowing what it was. She would continue to suffer depressions and anxiety all her life but never blamed her mother, who she said 'did nothing bad' to her and in many respects was a good mother. As an adult she could see that living with a depressive mother would make for a worried child, and that a child would blame itself because unable to understand where the unhappiness was coming from. As an adolescent she would continue to struggle with the fact that adult life, too, seemed to be 'incredibly depressing'.

Schooling in Sheffield was at the junior department of Sheffield Girls High School, which Margaret didn't like: a bossy, highly regulated kind of school, she remembered, where she was annoyed to be made to finish the inedible dinners. At the age of thirteen she was sent to board at the ancient Mount School in York, run by the Quakers, where her mother had taught and where her sisters went also. Here Margaret was inspired with a love of English literature and theatre and did a little acting (alongside fellow pupil Judi Dench, who played the lead role of Titania in *A Midsummer Night's Dream* while the much younger Margaret played a fairy). The school made her 'not very good at self-promotion': the pupils were taught not to advertise themselves and to be careful of other people's feelings. There was an evening meditation to reflect on the day, no punishment of any sort – and therefore no power amongst the senior girls – and an ethos of respect for children and teachers. These were 'messages' that went very deep in her, Margaret was to comment. She was always top of the class, and eventually won a major scholarship to Newnham College in Cambridge. Kathleen pushed all three of her daughters to go to the women-only college to read English as she had done, and so each duly did: the pressure to follow their parents to university was 'unquestioned and intense, so intense that none of us actively rebelled against it. It seemed to be the only way to get away'. Margaret was never quite as confident as her mother that she would necessarily get there, however.

At Newnham she immediately felt at ease, finding a single-sex institution comfortable and relaxing, as she had at the Mount. But it was a new sort of existence:

I remember my first evening at Cambridge, people were talking about things that I didn't know about, and I was quite well educated and not totally socially inept, but still I felt there was a whole world here...

Amongst other revelations at university Margaret came upon Simone de Beauvoir's iconic feminist work *The Second Sex*, which argues that woman is always seen in relation to man and therefore as primarily a sexual being, and that a woman is forced to 'learn' how to be a woman and to adapt to a confined sphere ordained by men. To Margaret these new perceptions were wonderful and 'so important to me as a person'. She saw it as material that no one had as yet used, and knew that she was the one who could. However, writing was not the focus while she was a student; her chief interest was in performing. Because of the shortage of women actors she finally got to be Titania, and acted with future big names like Ian McKellen, Derek Jacobi, Eleanor Bron, and Trevor Nunn. Tragic heroine roles became her speciality.

She was 'very, very happy' at Cambridge, her depressions totally evaporating, and enjoying herself so much that 'it took me a long time to get over it'. The fun came at a price for some. In the 1950s all the young women students were terrified of getting pregnant, and naturally a few did. Margaret became aware that many would marry a man they didn't love rather than risk an abortion or social disgrace. 'Our generation knew there had to be a better way to live, only we couldn't work out what it was.'

The week Margaret left university with a first-class degree in 1960 she married the actor Clive Swift, later best known as Hyacinth Bucket's husband Richard in the television series *Keeping Up Appearances*. Margaret, just twenty-one, opted for a traditional white wedding in full-skirted white dress and short veil, and carrying a bouquet of white roses. Clive came from a large, noisy, generous, warm-hearted and loving family and she had fallen for all of them. 'I loved the Swifts,' Margaret said. 'They were so unlike the Drabbles.' She tried very hard to be a Swift, she remembered, but found there was always something dragging her back to be a Drabble.

Clive was already embarked on his professional career as an actor and at that point Margaret intended a life on the stage herself, but after a short period at the Royal Shakespeare Company playing minor non-speaking roles and understudying for Vanessa Redgrave, she found the ambition had dissipated – despite some good notices. She had had a baby in her first year of marriage and then another and then a third, and had begun to feel 'just a wife', even if knowing nothing about domestic matters or indeed birth control:

It was a different pattern then. Contraception wasn't all that brilliant. The pill hadn't been invented. I had my third child and then they invented the pill, otherwise I would probably have had a child a year.

Photograph: Edward Hamilton West

She enjoyed motherhood but in the gaps turned to writing as a career, wanting to do something expressive that could be fitted in around rearing small children. She produced her first book during her time in Stratford-upon-Avon and feeling very bored. Clive was working long hours at the theatre and she had no friends and nothing else to do; she nearly took a job, but tried her hand at writing instead. She was lucky enough to be accepted by the first publisher she approached (who no doubt recognised talent when they saw it). New women's magazines like *Cosmopolitan* and *Mademoiselle* were just starting to be published and there was a burgeoning market for women's fiction; there were many women like her, Margaret recalled, who wanted to read about what other women were doing. 'It hadn't yet reached the stage of being angry or very consciously feminist, it was just a feeling that "all is not quite right".' Her first two novels, perhaps influenced by the ideas of Simone de Beauvoir, investigated a modern woman's choices in a man's world

– career or marriage – while her play for television about a bored young graduate mother stuck at home with a baby, *Laura*, covered similar ground.

Somewhere along the line, with little domestic help and trying to write as well as care for her babies, Margaret began to feel 'rage' and desperation and was driven to take an overdose of paracetamol. She later denied that this was because, despite all the academic success and promise of her youth, she found herself in exactly the same situation as her mother, and indeed she was already an acknowledged writer of significant talent. Fortunately recovery followed, and she greatly regretted her action. Her children only became aware of this history through press reports many years later.

Her third novel, *The Millstone*, written while pregnant with her third child, has been seen as supplying the answer to the questions about career versus marriage that she was posing in the first two. This her most famous work, about an independent female academic who chooses single motherhood, was eventually translated into twenty languages and became a set text for schools. It has never been out of print, remains very popular to this day, and has been much studied – and identified with, despite Margaret's clever and well-off heroine hardly exemplifying the lot of many single mothers. (Margaret has even been accused of making the story much easier to write by removing all the normal obstacles a single mother has to overcome.)

But *The Millstone* is far from a simple book with a clear message.

§

In the novel Rosamund Stacey, an attractive young Cambridge graduate raised as a feminist and to think of herself as an equal to men, is writing a PhD thesis on early English poetry while living alone in her absent parents' spacious London flat. Her understanding about her own body is limited, and she is nervous about having sex – feeling 'apprehensive terror' at the very idea – but also reluctant in such modern times to divulge that she is still a virgin. For company and for camouflage she is stringing along two boyfriends who each think she is having sex with the other. Very much part of her avoidance of a real relationship is her inability at the start of the novel to open up to love and commitment, the 'bond that links man to man'. Then she meets BBC announcer George and is attracted to him, despite suspecting he is homosexual. There is a single, unpleasurable sexual encounter: George is also under the impression that she has two lovers, and is therefore unaware that this is in fact her first time. Afterwards Rosamund deliberately avoids seeing George and lets him disappear out of her life, in the ensuing months only occasionally listening to his voice on the radio. She is too shy, and unwilling to presume, to tell him that she has fallen in love with him.

Her convoluted thinking on the subject is indicative of the complexity of the novel. Asking for his address or phone number would have seemed an intrusion:

...an assumption that I had a right to know, that a future existed where it would be of use to know. I see, oh yes I see that my diffidence, my desire not to offend looks like enough to coldness, looks like enough to indifference, and perhaps I mean it to, but this is not what it feels like in my head. But I cannot get out and say, Where do you live, give me your

number, ring me, can I ring you? In case I am not wanted. In case I am tedious. So I let him go, without a word about any other meeting, though he was the one thing I wanted to keep...

The Millstone, Margaret Drabble, 1965

Discovering she is pregnant, Rosamund decides against telling either George or her parents and at first makes a half-hearted attempt at inducing a miscarriage with the traditional bottle of gin and hot bath. When this fails she resolves to go ahead with the pregnancy, and begins to feel confident that she can handle it all. To do so she withdraws into isolation, eschewing any possible help from friends and family and dismissing her two boyfriends. One of these, on being told of the pregnancy, asserts that all women want babies to give them a sense of purpose. Rosamund is incensed:

'What utter rubbish,' I said with incipient fury, 'what absolutely stupid reactionary childish rubbish. Don't tell me that any human being ever endured the physical discomforts of babies for something as vague and pointless as a sense of purpose.'

The Millstone, Margaret Drabble, 1965

For the first time in her hitherto healthy life, middle-class Rosamund, subsisting on a meagre income from academic grants and endowments, must make use of the National Health Service. In the antenatal clinic her eyes are opened to the lives of less fortunate women, representatives of a population whose existence she was barely aware of, and 'the impossible, heart-breaking uneven hardship of the human lot'. She suspects, rightly, that she too will now have to ask for help, and from strangers into the bargain; she feels her independence threatened. The pregnancy, she senses, may have been sent to her in order to reveal a way of living quite divorced from her previous selfish, self-sufficient existence. To her surprise, she begins to feel a kinship with the other mothers in the hospital antenatal clinic and joins in with her own family tales of harrowing births (although on one occasion also attempting to read an academic text as she waits to be seen, in one later critic's choice words 'an emblematic expression of the irreconcilable').

As the pregnancy slowly advances, and feeling sure that no potential adoptive parents could ever be the excellent mother that she will be, Rosamund continues her thesis in the hope that she can finish it before the birth. As far as she is concerned there is no reason why her proposed academic career should be interrupted. She simply did not believe that 'the handicap' of one tiny illegitimate child could make an iota of difference.

The labour and birth are then described – although without too much detail – the final stages depicted as violent but almost bordering on pleasure. The arrival of her daughter Octavia (named after the Victorian social reformer Octavia Hill) fills Rosamund with an unaccustomed tide of happiness: she is enraptured. It is love that she feels, she finally recognises, 'the first of my life', and is constantly astonished by the way she can gaze for hours at Octavia's every tiny movement and facial expression:

I certainly had not anticipated such wreathing, dazzling gaiety of affection from her whenever I happened to catch her eye...Indeed, it must have been in expectation of this love that I had insisted upon having her.

The Millstone, Margaret Drabble, 1965

When the baby is a few months old and diagnosed with a congenital heart defect requiring surgery, Rosamund experiences dread and grief on behalf of someone else – again, for the first time – and knows that she too is now vulnerable to the evils of chance. She obediently delivers her daughter for treatment but when refused permission to visit, as was then still common with hospitalised children, she starts deliberately screaming and continues to do so until the annoyed staff allow her access – but only after the intervention of a doctor friend. Meeting other mothers of ill children in the hospital, Rosamund is made aware that most will lack the self-confidence to get access as she has done (and who unlike her might not have a family friend as their child's doctor).

The arrival of daughter Octavia, and all that Rosamund has experienced, has meant an end to her isolation from the rest of the human race. She has been forced to overcome her reluctance to ask for help because such reticence could affect her child, as when she must ask a neighbour to keep an eye on the baby while she runs out to the chemist's for antibiotics. Rosamund has learned to love and care, to connect with others. However, the final scene of the novel is a chance meeting with George, whom she invites up to the flat. She lies about Octavia's age so as not to enlighten him and thereby impose a sense of responsibility (although, in need of his support, she is tempted to reveal all); he leaves without understanding that he is the father. The novel therefore ends with Rosamund a new and loving mother, but one who is still pushing away the chance of an adult relationship. She is also publishing her thesis, has received an offer of a post at an attractive new university and has embarked on further poetical study. Her new academic title of Dr, she reflects, will go a long way towards obviating what she regards as the anomaly of her daughter's status.

§

This complex and multi-layered novel can be read on many levels, and indeed has been, but primarily as a groundbreaking assertion of dawning female independence – a statement that a woman can have it all, career *and* family, and without a man in support. It has also been viewed as a deliberate account of pregnancy, birth and motherhood when these defining experiences were rarely written about; and as a story of liberal guilt, about a middle-class, privileged girl feeling her way to understanding a different milieu. Some have seen it as describing the maturing of an isolated young woman as she becomes aware of her need for others, although with still a way to go, in that Rosamund rejects the idea of a man in her life and stops short of establishing any kind of real sisterhood with the other pregnant women she encounters.

How did Margaret Drabble herself explain the novel? Asked whether she was working out her own problems in her first three novels – all written in the first person, her only body of work in that format – she replied that almost inevitably an author would write about her particular age group and preoccupations. Certainly there are strong parallels with Margaret's personal experience, apart from unmarried pregnancy: she, too, had been 'unnaturally nervous' about sex when young (and then very eager to get on with it at the age of eighteen); she, too, had tasted the academic life and then young motherhood. Rosamund's reactions on meeting her baby for the first time were 'totally based' on Margaret's. She had been a rather surprised and reluctant mother, not wanting a baby and then thinking it wonderful as soon as she saw it: the 'default position' for many mothers, Margaret believed. And like the baby in *The Millstone*, one of her own children suffered heart problems, although she never had to leave the child alone in the hospital like her heroine (but believed she would have kicked up the same fuss if so). The plot was also influenced by Margaret knowing someone with a baby out of wedlock, as she did a real 'George' type working at the BBC.

However, producing a statement of emerging female independence was never her intention. For Margaret, Rosamund's single status was unimportant and not the crux of the novel at all. (When a Swedish magazine published the novel and altered the ending so that Rosamund and George get married, she was indignant at the fact of change but didn't really mind: at least they cared enough to want her characters to be happy. She also envisaged that ultimately Rosamund *would* marry in the years to come.) She later regretted not allowing Rosamund to reveal to George the secret of his paternity, which she felt he would have greeted with pleasure and commitment, and she considered that Rosamund had behaved badly in not being honest. She was alarmed to find that schoolgirls interpreted the novel as encouragement to have a child outside of marriage, when all the time she had been at particular pains to establish Rosamund's privileged background and permanent means of supporting herself. In her introduction to an edition for schools Margaret confirmed that her character's lack of a marriage ring was not the crucial factor:

The baby is an illegitimate baby, but to me, as I wrote it, I don't think that was the main point at all...In a sense the fact that the girl in the book isn't married is almost accidental...It was far more important to me that she was a lonely, proud and isolated person, and the fact that she wasn't married was simply an aspect of this loneliness.

There were aspects to Rosamund's character that reflected her creator's. Margaret later saw that she had been writing about different facets of herself turn and turn about: alternately strong and weak books, or a sad book followed by a comic book, a mirror to her manic-depressive swings of mood. There was something in her, said Margaret, that continually went between these two poles, and in writing her novels she was tossed from one to the other. The heroine in *The Millstone* she termed 'pretty defective', admitting that Rosamund's first words in the novel, that her career had always been marked by a strange mixture of confidence and cowardice, absolutely summed up Margaret herself.

For Margaret the point of *The Millstone* was not female independence, but the experience of motherhood:

I didn't have an agenda. It wasn't a political novel at all. It was about motherhood, because that was my life at the time. I wrote this one while I was expecting my third child and the book was very much about the experience of motherhood, maternity clinics, nurses, seeing the baby for the first time, and that was what I was writing about. It didn't really have a political view about the woman on her own, it just turned out that way.

Margaret said that she wrote the book 'to solve the problem of why something that is so disagreeable and humiliating and at times painful and frightening [to have a child] should also be so important and rewarding'. Motherhood gives a strange mixture of freedom and responsibility which you find difficult to imagine until you have a child, she observed, and considerably changes your personality and perceptions. What she actually wanted to write about was the experience of maternity, the amazing delight she felt in her own first baby – and how maternity 'changes you into something fiercer than you were before'. Thus Rosamund starts off lonely, isolated and proud, but through motherhood is slowly humanised.

In her subsequent novels and other writing Margaret's focus on the experience of motherhood was to earn her the title 'novelist of maternity'. She saw motherhood in such positive terms it was almost an embarrassment to state it, she once said. 'I think it's the greatest joy in the world.' Her model was not her parent but her mother-in-law Mrs Swift, who created a demonstrably loving home in stark contrast to that of the inhibited Drabbles.

Far from making a feminist point Margaret also thought that in writing the book she was part of the mainstream, not saying anything particularly new about the importance of having both work and children. She was surprised that more people weren't saying the same thing, but just assumed that her meaning was obvious – only realising later that it was not so obvious, and that she had actually done something 'rather brave'. Now, in maturity, she still does not think any of the problems raised by having both a career and motherhood are soluble, but can see that her novel at least highlighted the question and that her character Rosamund solved it in her own way.

§

Contemporary critics did not quite know how to take *The Millstone*, with its many layers and jostling ideas. The book came out in 1965, two years before the Abortion Act of 1967, and inevitably sparked some indignation in response to the frank account of Rosamund's attempt to abort the pregnancy. When the novel was read aloud on BBC radio there was criticism from listeners – surprising to Margaret, as her character had not succeeded and had gone on to have the baby, although she understood that this too might have been offensive because Rosamund was not married. Margaret explained on *Woman's Hour* that to her mind Rosamund had behaved perfectly responsibly.

Most were impressed with the work (incidentally the first novel in Europe to be printed by computer) and in 1966 it brought Margaret the John Llewellyn Rhys Memorial Prize. As with her initial two novels, Margaret was acclaimed at the time for writing in a way that was new and hugely influential: about the real experience of attempted abortion, childbirth and motherhood. Almost universally the title was taken to mean that the baby was a millstone, an encumbrance, but Margaret was to clarify that she was also referring to Jesus' words in the Bible on the sin of harming children: 'whoso shall offend one of these little ones…it were better for him that a millstone were hanged about his neck, and that he were drowned in the depth of the sea'. It was a double image, she elucidated, the millstone both as burden and as punishment for neglecting a child, although perhaps not used as such entirely intentionally: 'The more I questioned it, the less I knew why I had chosen it.'

As to the actual message of the novel, however, critical opinions differed. Margaret Drabble in her admirably written third novel had created a 'self-righteous' unmarried mother, said the *Times*, noting with approval the way the author had created the traces of pedantry in Rosamund's voice which you would expect of a thesis-writing girl fresh out of university, and likewise the equally expected class consciousness of a would-be classless young woman like Rosamund. However, the paper's critic saw a disappointing lack of thought behind Margaret's apparent theme of the single mother supposedly defying society. 'Miss Drabble's concern is really only for what the neighbours will think, and her moral stand is how fine it is to defy them.' There was no consideration of what life would be like for the fatherless child, the review continued, no ethical evaluation of Rosamund's deliberate avoidance of marriage, and no explanation of the inadequacy of all the male characters.

A second *Times* review of the novel, on the other hand, summed it up as 'Very funny, very moving; not to be missed'. The *Times Literary Supplement*, for its part (and with perhaps better understanding of at least some of what Margaret Drabble intended), observed that *The Millstone* was not just a tale about unmarried pregnancy but rather the story of the awakening of a person, the heightening of perceptions and the softening of attitudes. Rosamund, to start with a 'self-satisfied prig', became utterly convincing.

Whatever critics thought about the novel, readers devoured it, and continue to do so in the twenty-first century. It remains Margaret Drabble's bestselling work in the UK, ploughing through more reprints than any one of her others.

§

The film of *The Millstone* was directed by Waris Hussein, director of the opening episode of *Dr Who* on TV in 1963. It was his first feature film, appearing in 1969 as *A Touch of Love*, the title changed from the original for commercial reasons. Margaret adapted the novel for the screen herself in her one and only screenplay. As might be expected, therefore, the plot closely follows that of the novel. Waris commented that Margaret in writing the screenplay followed her instincts with great integrity and brought humour to the dialogue.

American actress Sandy Dennis played the lead part, successfully mastering a middle-class English accent. Eleanor Bron was in the role of the heroine's friend while a very young Ian McKellen played the effeminate George – and believed himself to be the real original of George in the novel. Margaret made clear that the character was based on an actual BBC newsreader, however. Both Waris and Ian had been friends of Margaret's at Cambridge.

The film could not have been financed without a big name like Sandy's and for Waris she was a very necessary but admittedly 'idiosyncratic' lead. As far as Ian McKellen was concerned Sandy's acting was 'full of not very convincing mannerisms...she was pretending to make it up as she went along', and in a public discussion of the film many years later he wryly complimented Waris on his capable excision of Sandy's quirks. Ian also thought the role should have been played more militantly, but for the director this would not have sustained the film as he believed the character needed to be fragile. Sandy herself, of course, was a 'dear' and 'lovely', said Ian.

Sandy was indeed frequently described as neurotic and mannered in her performances, and had been dubbed 'Our Lady of the Nervous Tics' and even 'Dennis the Menace' by American critics. She would run words together, stop and start sentences, suddenly change octave as she spoke and flutter her hands – becoming unforgettable as an actress in the process. A *New York Times* critic referred to her sentences on stage as 'poor crippled things that couldn't cross a street without making three false starts from the kerb'. Some of this is evident in the film, and she also spends a lot of time playing with her lifeless hair, but for some she still convinced as Rosamund. Sandy revealed decades later that some years before playing the part of a pregnant girl and new mother in *A Touch of Love* she and her then partner, the jazz musician Gerry Mulligan, had suffered a miscarriage. She commented that if she had given birth she would have loved the child, but that she didn't feel any connection with it when pregnant. 'I never, ever wanted children. It would have been like having an elephant.' Nevertheless, she claimed *A Touch Of Love* as her favourite film.

The film was entered into the Berlin International Film Festival but failed to win any awards. It was a flop at the box office in the UK and equally so in the US, where like the American edition of the novel it appeared as *Thank You All Very Much,* a reference to Rosamund's politely sarcastic response to a group of medical students who examine her without speaking to her or acknowledging her as a person. While not a box office success the film reportedly still made a profit, as the filmmakers sold it to the distributors for more than its cost.

As for the critics, the *Times* saw it as an old-fashioned weepie, a little 'roughly directed' by Waris Hussein, but written from a remarkably accurate observation of speech and behaviour in a certain graduate milieu. The *Illustrated London News*, for some reason, reacted mainly with a vehement denunciation of the portrayal of the NHS. Its reviewer was 'astonished at the bitterness of the film's attack on our medical welfare system': the heroine treated with offensive brusqueness by a GP receptionist in front of a crowded waiting room, in hospital placed in the wrong bed in the wrong ward, and subsequently ignored by three idly chatting nurses oblivious to her screams of pain. A 'callously insensitive' Sister tells her how selfish it is to keep her child when it could so easily be adopted.

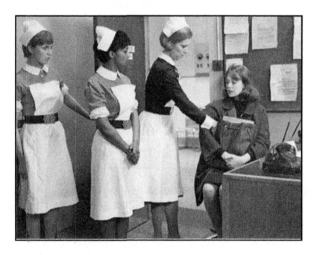

Taken together, these scenes provided a ludicrously exaggerated picture of an unfeeling and almost inhuman Health Service, thundered the review. The acting was well done, it conceded, particularly Ian McKellen's 'fascinating ambisextrous portrayal' of the lover, but the central relationships would have been more convincing had Miss Drabble painted a 'less vicious portrait of the treatment meted out to expectant, unmarried mothers'. The *Reading Evening Post* took the same tack, although better able to grasp that this was not in fact an unrealistic depiction – women herded together like cattle, kept hanging about for hours, and treated with disdain by haughty nursing sisters more concerned with the smooth running of their wards than with patients' emotional well-being. There was undoubtedly some truth in such scenes, said the *Post*, but the film failed to take into account the difficulties faced by the NHS in trying to cope with huge numbers of women with inadequate staff and hospital facilities.

Across the Atlantic the *New York Times* was mostly in favour, finding the film disciplined, good-humoured, thoughtful and 'often very beautiful', even if deeming the plotline basically banal and melodramatic. A woman's picture, the reviewer declared: some smiles, some tears, the events and objects of daily living, a little sex and a little chastity – but at the same time a film a little more feminist than romantic, given its assumption that without being Greta Garbo a woman might reasonably choose to live alone. Sandy Dennis, though still displaying tricks, ticks and grimaces, was judged more controlled than usual, while Ian McKellen brought to his role as the probably bisexual young BBC newscaster exactly the right quality of 'flexible shy elegance'.

Ian McKellen went on to a glittering acting career and so did Sandy, who was bisexual and later had a chapter devoted to her in Boze Hadleigh's *Hollywood Lesbians*. She became more interested in animals than her own image ('I should have kept myself blonder and thinner, but I just didn't care enough') and was a renowned animal activist, rescuing stray cats from the depths of Grand Central Station in New York. At the time of her very early death from ovarian cancer aged fifty-four, she was living with more than twenty of her rescued animals.

§

Margaret Drabble became one of the most successful novelists of her time, in subsequent years often labelled a writer of 'Hampstead novels' for her focus on the lives of anguished intelligentsia. Forever after associated with Britain's fledgling feminism, she consistently created heroines forced to contend with domestic life and the imposed limitations of being female, always conflicted by the claims of maternity, sexuality and intellectual or economic aspiration, but with the joy of children some compensation. Her later novels became broader in range, their focus more on documenting social change in a Britain she saw as increasingly in decline, and critics began to accuse her of being outmoded. 'I've been around too long and was doing too nicely and they don't like that.' She remains unapologetic about her unwavering espousal of Northern values, traditional writing, and her particular brand of realism, and continues in the same vein; she remains a highly respected and award-winning writer, biographer, and critic. When editor of the 1985 edition of the *Oxford Companion to English Literature*, entries for women writers rose considerably, and included all of the writers in the present book with the exception of herself (although allowing an entry when editor again in 2000). She is a Dame Commander of the Order of the British Empire.

As the novels kept coming Margaret's mother Kathleen applauded her daughter's success. Her state of mind had greatly improved with appropriate medication, and with each new book she wrote Margaret a congratulatory and appreciative letter (until about the twelfth, according to Margaret, when the ageing Kathleen felt she could no longer keep it up). Relations with her sister and rival novelist Antonia Byatt remain famously strained, not least because of autobiographical elements in their work which cause tension, each resenting the use of common material by the other. Margaret has described the situation as normal sibling rivalry, with Antonia agreeing that the issue is 'terribly overstated by gossip columnists'. Antonia has also stated that they would help each other 'at the last ditch' – although adding maybe not at the first ditch. Margaret admits that it has been a very complicated relationship:

I published first and I was younger which is, of course, annoying. Then she won the Booker, which evened things up a bit. Then she got made a dame, then I got made a dame. It's ridiculous, it's like some sort of comedy. Death is the next thing so I suppose that's the next battle!

Margaret and Clive Swift divorced in 1975 because Margaret was having an affair, which then continued for some years. In the 1980s she began a relationship with the biographer Michael Holroyd, whom she later married, although for a long time they kept separate homes – both 'absolutely love' being alone but also greatly enjoy each other's company and wanted to have it both ways. They now live together, writing in different parts of the same house and meeting up at the end of their working day. They employ an imaginary butler called Peel, sometimes played by Michael. Margaret has reservations about the married state:

I think marriage is a dangerous, dangerous relationship, full of potential destruction of personality. People aren't meant to be together twenty-four hours a day. The form of relationship we have seems much more natural.

She met fellow 'Angry Young Woman' Nell Dunn when Nell won the John Llewellyn Rhys Memorial prize for *Up the Junction*; they became firm friends when both on a writers' tour in 1969, travelling around the country doing readings and discussions. Margaret thought Nell 'very disarming' and always looked lovely with her freckles, abundant, fair curly hair and floaty long skirts. (Margaret herself favoured rather short skirts.) Later the two would go and stay with each other with their children, or go to plays together. Margaret saw Nell as a 1960s figure, slightly bohemian and colourful without being wildly eccentric: approachable, unshockable, and with an amazing capacity for getting on with people from all social classes. There was something unconstructed about Nell's way of looking at the world, said Margaret, a sort of faux-naïve quality which was very hopeful. She thought Nell lucky not to have had a formal literary education as it had given her 'an extraordinary freshness of eye and ear'.

The two once laughed over an incident in a restaurant when a waiter told the fine-cheekboned, wispy-haired Nell that she looked like a writer; Nell, indicating Margaret with her severe and practical bob, responded that her friend was a writer too. 'She looks like a housewife,' said the waiter.

§

Regarding her current mental equilibrium, Margaret says of herself that she lives in a state of acute anxiety, with things 'festering inside'. But she has found ways of dealing with the depressions she has suffered since childhood. 'I've never taken anti-depressants because the intensity of my feeling makes me write.' She calms herself with jigsaws and walks on the moors behind her house in Somerset to enjoy the sky and the birds, sometimes visiting a church where her plea (not prayer) harks back to her Quaker upbringing: Let me be a better self.

As for writing, Margaret Drabble describes it as 'an illness. A chronic, incurable illness. I caught it by default when I was twenty-one, and I often wish I hadn't.' Her subject has mainly been the lives of women and the way they are bound together. 'Women are not exempt from rivalry and ambition but there is something in the circumstances of their lives that gives them a common bond,' she observed. She has hesitated to use the term feminist to describe herself, claiming that her aim was only ever to reflect the female experience. 'That's how life was...It's realism, not feminism.' Ultimately, however, she became less equivocal:

Now, I do consider myself a feminist. I'm not a militant – I don't go to meetings or marches – but I've always believed in equal rights.

Looking back at the success and longevity of *The Millstone*, Margaret realised that she was writing in a 'very fortunate' period, in which many young women like her were discovering the same kinds of problems and also having the same kind of doors opening for them. She came to feel that she was writing for a generation, and had been lucky to find a large readership. She went from feeling quite lonely and believing that her experience was isolated, to understanding how in fact her experience linked up with that of many other people. It was a matter of timing, she commented: in the early 1960s the women's movement had yet to get going but 'obviously the people who were going to move within it were already thinking the things that they were thinking'. Since that point strides had been made, said Margaret in 2016. Compared to the lives of her mother's generation, which were full of disappointment and frustration, 'and anger, frankly', women now had far more outlets to express their ire. Progress had been made but more was needed. Feminism had not reached its goals, in her opinion – the salary gap was huge – but on the other hand there was now maternity and paternity leave and certain rights were now accepted that never were when she was young. She therefore saw it as a narrative of progress. There had been a huge evolution of women's thinking, and it had been a great time to be a writer.

Margaret certainly used the word feminist when reflecting on her 2011 complete collection of short stories *A Day in the Life of a Smiling Woman*, which stretch in time from the early Sixties to the start of the new century. They present a kind of social history in which the female characters in each story become gradually older, ranging from a young bride to new mothers to merry widows. The men are uniformly awful: condescending, pathetic, miserly, or just useless. One is actually dead, much to his widow's relief. Interviewed in connection with the publication of the stories – in an article entitled 'The original angry young woman' – Margaret commented:

I was surprised by how angry some of the middle stories were. They were quite feminist and I was a bit surprised because I hadn't thought they were. I thought that was what everybody was thinking. And in fact, everybody was. Women were thinking like that; it wasn't just me.

But what she hoped most, declared Margaret a few years later, was that her writing might have made life easier and more fun for women, and that they found in her work both optimism and companionship.

Georgy Girl

Margaret Forster

She didn't see how she could ever stop looking like a caricature. It was something to do with her face being too long and big and her damned hair being the way it was. As ever, she struggled with herself not to give way to self-pity. She had to try to alter herself. Pushing to the back of her mind a vivid picture of all the other times she'd had a 'Resurrect George' campaign, she bit her lip, frowned, and wondered what she could do.

Georgy Girl, Margaret Forster, 1965

Georgy burst upon the scene in 1965, an unlikely heroine: tall, awkward, given to clowning, and slightly depressed. But in the 1966 film of the novel, and as embodied in the accompanying catchy, upbeat song *Georgy Girl*, she was depicted as something quite different: a free-spirited girl of the Swinging Sixties, and that is what she became – despite the fact that in appearance and behaviour Georgy of the original novel was very far from swinging, and in many ways actually at odds with 1960s values.

Georgy, as conceived by Margaret Forster (or George, as she is called throughout the book except on one single occasion), is an awkward, virginal young woman on the outside of life looking in. It is her bitchy and promiscuous flatmate Meredith who is of the Sixties: a dolly bird, pretty and slender and throwing over all convention to live as she wants to. Georgy's subservient, blinkered, working-class parents work as valet and housekeeper for rich, middle-aged James, a man who wants statuesque Georgy to be his mistress. She avoids making any answer and, desperate for love and sex, falls for Meredith's boyfriend Jos. When Meredith becomes pregnant and decides to keep the baby – after four previous abortions – Jos does the decent thing and marries her, although fully aware of their complete lack of compatibility. Jos joins Meredith and Georgy in their seedy flat and after a while Georgy and Jos begin an affair. Meredith abandons her baby, Georgy's relationship with the basically irresponsible Jos falls apart and she is left with the child, whom she loves. Her parents' wealthy employer finally proposes marriage and, to give the baby a home, she accepts.

Georgy Girl is a mostly bleak novel, with nothing going right for Georgy pretty well all the way through, or indeed for any of the other characters. Georgy, full of affection for the children to whom she teaches dance, is depressed and emotional about what she perceives as her ugly appearance and her loneliness and lack of love. The relationship with Jos soon fails and she is never attracted to the thick-bodied James, either physically or as a person. But it all ends on an unexpectedly high note, with James taking a shine to the baby and promising Georgy some of her own. A friend at their wedding finally shows us the couple as they really are, and not as seen through Georgy's self-critical lens:

She studied James carefully...She was surprised he'd turned out so good looking. He was a bit fat, but not so that you couldn't call it heavy built. He was very straight backed with black hair, grey at the temples, and she thought he had a kind face. He was very smart.

[Georgy] looks ever so nice...They'd done something queer with her hair, twisted it all in coils on top of her head. Regal looking, that was the phrase. The dress was beautiful, high necked, long sleeved and masses of skirt...she was quite flushed...sort of pink. It was becoming.

Georgy Girl, Margaret Forster, 1965

The friend heads for home, thinking how happy Georgy must be about her big house and honeymoon and baby and perhaps more children to come, 'and how there was no knowing what might turn up for oneself'.

§

Margaret Forster was born in Carlisle in 1938, the middle child of working-class parents. At the time of her birth her taciturn father was working as a fitter at the Metal Box factory, going off to work each morning in his boiler suit; her nervous, self-sacrificing sensitive mother stayed at home to look after the family, consoling herself with religion. She lived a life of drudgery, in Margaret's opinion, rising before the sun to rake out and light the coal-fired stove, the home's only source of heating, then cooking, shopping, cleaning and hand-washing for her family of three children and receiving no remuneration for doing any of it. She had very high standards, even with such heavy work in an old-fashioned house: everything was always gleaming and artistically arranged, with jugs of fresh flowers. Home was a modest two-bedroomed council house with an outside toilet on the new Raffles estate on the outskirts of the city, followed by a move to a better place after the family had increased in size and the estate had degenerated. The infant Margaret, fiercely clever, talked in long sentences at the age of two and was a difficult child, noisy and demanding and given to tantrums. She never stopped asking questions and was reading and writing by the age of four; an impressed vicar helped in getting her admitted a year early to the infants' class at the local school. Here Margaret came into her own and could allow her real self to emerge – perfectly aware that she was not the sweet, compliant child her parents wanted, a domestic carer in the making. With her teachers she was bright and eager and expected to learn, not to wash up or bring the coal in as she was at home.

Witnessing her exhausted and depressed mother trapped at home in the traditional role, her life 'wasted, completely wasted', Margaret very early on resolved never to follow in her footsteps, much as she loved and admired her mother for her selflessness. Her mother had made one fatal mistake, the young Margaret reasoned: marrying and having children. For her the conclusion was obvious:

I would not marry and therefore would not have children. I would keep out of the trap and I'd be safe...The circumstances of my mother's life and her unhappiness were the spur to make my own life into something different. I would not and could not be like her.

She did not in any case want to bring children into the world, to be responsible for bringing another human being into such a terrible place. All the women she saw around her had hard lives, not just her mother. Life was bleak for everyone but it was women in particular who got up early and went out to a freezing cold washhouse to start the long laborious day, Margaret commented as an adult. To escape from this clearly required money, she saw. 'It was quite a simple equation.' She didn't want jewels or yachts or fur coats, just a different sort of existence. The means to achieve this was plainly through education, recently made more available to working-class girls through the 1944 Education Act, which for the first time ensured that all girls completed secondary schooling. She focused on her schoolwork and often refused to submit to her father's demands to help around the house, despite physical punishment. She read constantly, until sometimes having the book ripped from her hands by her furious parent, who also saw reading as a retreat from family life. 'Get your nose out of that book and help your mam, or else!' He raged against her disobedience,

Margaret recalled, but she was an inveterate, unrepentant reader and would remain so as long as she lived. (Her schoolgirl diaries reveal that in 1952, aged fourteen, she read 136 books and made critical comments in her diary about each one. In 1954, with exams coming up, she read 66.) As an adult Margaret would average a book a day, and not surprisingly her knowledge of books and plays was vast. In her girlhood at home, however, where there were no books, there could be no discussion about her discoveries:

Trying to talk about the contents of books was showing off and there was no need for it. My reading was seen as a weapon I used against my family, a way of absenting myself from their company. 'All she does is that damned reading,' my father complained, and it was true. It made me strange to them.

As she grew older the relationship with her father remained precarious. Margaret criticised him freely, the way he ate, the way he spoke, how he came home from work in the evenings and washed himself at the kitchen sink. It was revolting, she told him, leaving the room even in the middle of a meal to get away from the sight.

Winning a place at the respected Carlisle and County High School for girls – after weeks of nightmares as she awaited the results of her exam, desperate to avoid repeating her mother's fate – Margaret pushed herself to excel there. (She was so bent on academic progress that she once famously petitioned the headmistress *not* to grant a half-day holiday when Arsenal came to play Carlisle United at the local football ground, the biggest game in the club's history. Cinema newsreel showed the ground full to bursting and the town centre deserted.) Her parents worried that she would get 'above herself', making her unfit for what they saw as a woman's role. But such a role was not what Margaret wanted, 'hard and selfish and strange' as it seemed to her family. Her rebelliousness in her teenage years took the form of dressing all in black, cropping her long wavy hair brutally short and refusing to wear high heels and nylons like everyone else (suspender belts were 'like harnesses', she complained, and she wasn't a horse). She wanted to look different, to be set apart from her mother and other women and girls in Carlisle. She didn't want what they wanted, 'some kind of pleasant job for a few years until Mr Right came along'.

Her father made her life a misery, demanding to know why she didn't wear nice frocks or a decent coat:

My appearance, while I was growing up, was endlessly commented on and always critically. I was getting fat (though 'fat' was a euphemism for 'developing') and it didn't suit me; my hair looked as if a mouse had chewed it and it made me look like a lad; my spots were all barnacles (though, in fact, I hardly ever had even a small spot)...

As an adolescent she naturally became interested in sex and began to wonder about contraception, though well before the point she needed any. She was determined never to take the risk of getting pregnant and ending up trapped like her mother, but was unclear how to prevent it. Books were the only way to find out and Margaret spent some furtive hours flipping through medical texts in the library, where eventually she came upon the works of birth control campaigner Marie Stopes and gained some insights. There were clearly devices available which could prevent babies, she realised, and resolved to be fitted with one when the time came:

No boy, no amount of passion...was going to impregnate me and spoil my ambitious plans. My mother, my aunts, they had made the fatal mistake of being trapped by children, and I wasn't going to.

The vital thing was to be independent, to be single-minded, to have a goal and allow no distractions.

University became a possibility. For the ambitious Margaret it was Oxford or Cambridge or nothing, which to her baffled family was downright selfishness and showing off. Menial Saturday and summer jobs, including at a hot and noisy steam laundry sorting dirty clothes alongside foul-mouthed fellow workers, only served to confirm her determination to live a different life. She could not understand why the other girls around her did not feel the same. 'Why weren't they all, as I was, raging and burning to have lives other than those of the women we knew?' she asked. A summer stint at Marks & Spencer, however, opened up a different sort of vista. Margaret was astounded at how clean and well organised it was behind the scenes at the store, with its excellent canteen and hair salon for staff. The only boring part was the actual work serving behind the counters.

Escape finally beckoned when she was accepted both at Cambridge and at Oxford, where she chose to read modern history. Leaving Carlisle behind her, in 1957 Margaret set off for Somerville College.

§

She hated it. She found the university oppressive, and couldn't fit in. The intellectual life that Margaret had so hoped would spare her a life of domestic drudgery bored her to death, and actually seemed a form of gross self-indulgence when compared with the reality of most women's lives. It felt wrong. Nevertheless, she worked conscientiously, and easily produced the brilliant essays and ideas in tutorials the university demanded (if chafing at the way the constraints of writing very balanced essays ran contrary to her instinctive flow). But her heart was not in it: she didn't really care, and finally recognised that essentially she was too frivolous.

It was not all bad. She loved her scholar's gown, a long affair worn by those who had won scholarships to distinguish them from the other undergraduates, and wore it everywhere. She loved meeting fellow students called Theodora and Annabel and Henrietta – without any sense of inferiority or dents to her self-confidence – girls from a different environment who had never met anyone quite like Margaret before and who gently influenced her taste, weaning her away from Woolworths plates and candlewick bedspreads to mismatched china and Afghan covers. Most of all, after years of sharing her bedroom with her sister, she loved having a room of her own. Because she was a scholar she had one of the best rooms in Somerville, large and square and overlooking a lawn and cedar trees.

Through her teachers and the mothers of her new friends Margaret also for the first time came into contact with educated women, professional middle-class intellectuals who were happily balancing careers and children, and it gradually occurred to her that if she earned enough money then she, too, might be able to have it all and get to enjoy every aspect of a woman's life if she found she wanted to. 'I didn't know, before then, that you could be like that.' She came into contact too with contemporaries who knew about birth control and abortion, and on their advice made an appointment to be fitted with a Dutch cap – triumphantly telling the Family

Planning Clinic, when they asked when she was getting married, that she wasn't. There would be no illegitimate babies for Margaret, as there had been for her grandmother and great-grandmother; if ever she did have an unplanned pregnancy then she would simply get an abortion, illegal though it still was in the late 1950s. 'Why...did everyone stress the importance of the vote for women when control over their own bodies matters so much more?' was her question.

Margaret at this point was already committed to her longtime Carlisle boyfriend (and later Beatles biographer) Hunter Davies, with whom she had once gone to see John Osborne's play *Look Back in Anger*.

They first met as teenagers, when Hunter asked Margaret at a youth club if she fancied a dance. 'Certainly not,' she replied before stalking off. 'In fact there's nothing I would like less. I hate dancing.' Hunter did not get another chance for about two years, although hearing plenty about her. He was a student working as a ticket collector on the Ribble buses when she got on as a passenger and, in an effort to impress, Hunter offered her a free ride. True to form Margaret refused to cheat the system and insisted on handing over her fare, later getting off without a backward glance. Eventually they got together after Margaret had finished her A levels. They hiked and biked around her beloved Cumbria, she the one usually carrying the rucksack.

Hunter wondered what 'such a blue stocking, clever, original, talented, forthright, strong-willed girl' saw in him, and was even more impressed the day her A level results came through:

Distinctions in English and History, plus a pass in Latin. The High School headmistress, Miss Cotterell, sent her actual marks in English and History, which were 95% in each, unheard of for those sort of art subjects.

Her father gave her a ten-shilling note to celebrate – a source of amazement to both Hunter and Margaret, knowing that he did not believe in girls' education. After Margaret graduated from Oxford in 1960 they married so that they could live together, which in those days meant a wedding to keep the families happy. (Previously, when spending a summer with Hunter at his digs in Manchester, Margaret even in her twenties had had to enlist friends to send her parents letters from Italy where she was supposedly on holiday with a girlfriend.) Their union was to last her lifetime, despite the rocky start when first going out with each other. There had been violent arguments, often about minor issues such as Hunter's lack of punctuality, and in his memory often ending in screams and shouts and stormings-off from Margaret. But he remained impressed by her clear, logical mind and propensity for analysis of other people's thinking, a process which to him usually seemed to arrive at the worst possible conclusions. One of her pessimistic predictions early on was that she was bad for Hunter, bringing him down and making him upset, and that therefore they ought to part. Luckily, Hunter was more sanguine, and presumably these stormy beginnings worked themselves out in the end. Margaret in later life proudly admitted to never having had any lover other than her husband, a record she compared to the Queen's. She had never been remotely attracted to anyone else, she said.

Marriage, of course, hardly fitted with Margaret's vision of a life distinct from that of her parents, but she ensured that the wedding was not in her words a 'charade' and the 'height of hypocrisy', but instead as untraditional as she could make it – a registry office ceremony wearing a simple white cotton dress, no bridesmaids, no parents invited and no reception, although she did invest in a fetching going-away outfit of lilac fitted jacket and skirt. As registry office weddings do not include the word 'obey' in the service, Margaret did not have to ask for it to be removed. She had been much incensed, as an 11-year-old bridesmaid at a church wedding, to hear the bride promising to obey but not the husband. When she declared that she would never use the word herself, her church-going mother responded that then she would never be a wife – leaving the young Margaret perfectly satisfied.

Now that she *had* married, her parents were disturbed by what seemed to them a furtive way of going about it and upset, naturally, that after all that education she was simply throwing herself away. There had been interesting opportunities not taken as she finished her studies: a promising job at the BBC, for one. After sailing through two interviews for their very selective graduate training scheme, Margaret had innocently scuppered her chances by telling them she was about to marry – frowned upon as it was assumed that young married women would inevitably get pregnant and leave. She had also turned down the offer of a job from *Woman's Own* on the strength of an article she had written defending women's magazines, and likewise a suggestion from her tutor that she stay on at Oxford and do research. Margaret knew what she *didn't* want to do, and felt perfectly sure she would somehow make her way.

She chose instead to embark upon what was to be her life's work: writing, her new ambition after earlier yearnings to be a missionary or an MP. (Growing up in Carlisle there had been no author role models to inspire her in this direction; all the writers she was aware of were dead.) For three months she sat at home writing her first attempt at a novel, initially in longhand and then laboriously typed out with two fingers. This was a sprawling, Dickensian-type story with an 'appalling, pretentious title' (*Green Dusk For Dreams*) which she sent off to a young agent. The agent suggested some revisions and requested a meeting, but the impatient Margaret took this for just a carefully couched rejection and immediately gave up being a novelist. She concentrated instead on her sensible job as a supply teacher at a girls' secondary modern school near Pentonville prison in London. She made good friends amongst the other staff and became an excellent teacher to her difficult, unruly classes, enthusiastic and energetic and able to discipline. The girls had all failed the 11-plus and had low expectations; Margaret tried to 'raise' them and would be remembered very fondly for her inspiring English lessons.

After a few months, however, she slowly returned to writing, deciding this time to write about what she knew. Her mood was 'slightly sulky' after her first brush with authorship and she chose as her subject something easy, 'one of those light books that seemed to be popular'. The result was *Dames' Delight*, written in the evenings after school and at weekends, the storyline an almost exact mirror of her experience as a student: gutsy young working-class girl escapes to Oxford but is bored and repelled by the repressed women students and idiotic, entitled males – and by the emphasis on sex, so much at odds with Margaret's own values. *Dames' Delight*, published by Jonathan Cape in 1964, successfully launched Margaret's career as a novelist, giving her the confidence to give up teaching and concentrate on writing: 'It wasn't a good novel but at least it got me started.'

She also began to think about having a family, although up till now she had felt 'no maternal urge'. This seemed brave and daring after all the earlier misgivings. 'It was very strange, the discovery that I could experience this odd physical sensation of suddenly craving a baby.' She had at first resisted Hunter's desire for a family (at least six), feeling herself not up to the job like her selfless mother – too irritable and demanding. Then she gradually fell in love with the idea of creating something that would be a product of their combined genes, and could see their child, always a boy. Her next novel, *Georgy Girl*, was written during a happy, easy pregnancy and when the baby arrived – a daughter – Margaret was instantly passionate. Thereafter she couldn't bear to miss a single second and refused to leave the baby in anyone else's care. 'She became a rival for Hunter, and I always put the baby first, not him.' A son was to follow (not the easiest of children) and then another girl when Margaret started to feel broody again and was unable to resist.

Her heroine Georgy was never meant to be any kind of icon of the times: the point of the novel for its author was her character's great love for children. Georgy had pleaded with Meredith not to abort her previous pregnancies and once the baby is born Georgy becomes obsessed:

Really, she hadn't guessed how she would react to Sara either, even though she had thought so much about her. She had never imagined love for a baby, especially a baby that wasn't yours, could be so strong and emotional. When she'd held her for the first time, there was a physical sensation not unlike one of desire. The same weak feeling in her stomach, the same breathless anticipation.

Georgy Girl, Margaret Forster, 1965

Margaret actually compared Georgy to her own mother in this respect, in a different time and place, with a different personality, but trading everything for babies. She knew that her mother had married only to have a family (and not, apparently, out of love for her father), and in this she was akin to Georgy whom Margaret described as 'a woman obsessed with having children, that's all she wanted out of life'. Many women married mainly in order to create a family, Margaret believed. Georgy's flatmate Meredith, on the other hand, was having a baby she didn't want and had no maternal feelings whatsoever, an occasional female trait that

Margaret was intrigued by and was frequently to write about.

That the novel is essentially about Georgy's desire for a baby is not immediately obvious – the first part of the story revolves around her desperation for love and sex. But Margaret's clarification does explain what is clearly meant to be a happy ending, with Georgy getting to keep Meredith's child and marrying with the promise of more to come (even if to a man she does not love, like Margaret's mother). However, other elements of the work hit exactly the right note for the Sixties: three young people living unconventionally together in a flat, shifting partners amongst themselves and defying parental expectations and societal norms. A new family unit is created when Meredith and Jos both reject their child and Georgy takes on the role of mother – and James of father – because they want to: the message seems to be that families are made, not born, and can be better for it. These new ideas were in tune with the spirit of the times and the novel was a success, not only chiming with a younger audience but also receiving plaudits from more traditional sources. 'A deliciously wry approach,' commented the *Evening Standard*. Easy to read and 'thoroughly likeable', approved the *Tatler*. 'Real talent here.' For the *Observer* the novel was caustic and highly readable, although the *Times Literary Supplement* damned it as slapdash and for the *Sunday Times* it was a faithful attempt at describing the 'egocentric idiocy of warring women'.

But it was the film that transmogrified Georgy into the rebellious Sixties icon that she ultimately became.

§

The film rights sold quickly and the film itself was eventually backed by American company Columbia. The contract for the rights stipulated that Margaret write the film script, despite the fact that she was completely inexperienced in the art of screenwriting and also four months pregnant with her second baby. For the rights to the novel and her work on the screenplay Margaret received £3,000, then a fortune.

It soon became clear that she was not cut out for the work, and would always put her family before the demands of the film:

One thing writing for myself, at home, quite another writing to orders, other people's orders...How clearly this episode showed me the limits of my own energies. Being a novelist fitted in with motherhood, being a scriptwriter didn't.

Her husband Hunter's first book *Here We Go Round the Mulberry Bush* was also being turned into a film at the time and their house hummed with meetings – directors, producers, actors – a situation which Margaret thoroughly disliked, even though people were in fact meeting at the house to save her coming to them in her state of advanced pregnancy and later, new motherhood. The producer would talk about *film noir* and wanted long, intellectual discussions, driving Margaret mad. It was hardly a workman-like atmosphere for them, she knew, discussing business in a room full of toys and baby clothes to the accompaniment of roars from new baby Jake (delivered early by Hunter, who had to disentangle the cord around Jake's neck). But they were tolerant, sitting with their scripts on their knees and making suggestions for changes which Margaret suffered impatiently, well aware she was no team player. In the end the task was handed over to

Peter Nichols, then a fairly new playwright, and both their names appeared in the credits. Peter spent three weeks revising the script and in later years labelled the result 'a bit of 1960s camp about a fat girl who finds love'. At a preview of the film the director asked him who the hell was going to pay to see it. 'All the fat girls?' suggested Peter.

The part of Georgy was given to twenty-three-year-old Lynn Redgrave, sister of the more famous Vanessa, who had originally accepted the part herself but pulled out a week or so before shooting was due to start. Lynn had auditioned for the role of Georgy's friend living in the flat below, in the novel an overweight and charmless character who plays little part in the proceedings. The director had always had his doubts about Vanessa's rightness for the role, and thought they had cast the wrong sister. 'Vanessa was the beautiful Greta Garbo of the Sixties,' he acknowledged, wondering how she could ever have been made to look like the back of a bus as seemingly demanded by Margaret's story (a superficial reading of the novel, as it is made clear that Georgy has her attractions). When Vanessa withdrew, the director offered Lynn the lead instead, despite the American producer hankering after big (ill-fitted) names to play the part. Lynn was uncomfortable about taking the role from her sister, although she too had secretly wondered how Vanessa was going to manage to look 'ungainly and lumpy' as apparently required. She called Vanessa to clear it with her, admitting later that she had sought Vanessa's 'permission and approval'. Vanessa had always hated the script and told Lynn it was a load of old rubbish, but wished her great success. Their mother, actress Rachel Kempson, was also to play a small part in the film.

James Mason played Georgy's wealthy older admirer James and a young Alan Bates was Jos, kitted out in full Sixties style with Donovan cap, floral shirts and Beatles haircut. Bill Owen, later Compo in TV's *Last of the Summer Wine*, played Georgy's father. Charlotte Rampling, new on the acting scene, played the brutal Meredith in a series of stunning Mary Quant outfits.

Because she was unused to children and was supposed to have a baby in the film the producer insisted Charlotte visit Margaret and practise with the real thing (although as the story demands that she be downright hostile to babies she would hardly have been expected to know what to do with one). Charlotte also did not understand her character and wanted some insights from the author, not seeing how someone like Margaret, surrounded by babies, could have imagined a woman with no maternal feelings. Margaret explained that the pregnancy was not planned, that Meredith had not been satisfying any maternal urge and would naturally resent the baby and the pain and trouble it brought her.

Charlotte Rampling did not seem very comfortable during the visit, Hunter remembered: rather cool and austere. He and heavily pregnant Margaret also visited the set at Shepperton Studios, where they found Lynn Redgrave far more friendly and natural and more interested in children.

It was the first starring part for Lynn, who had recently appeared in the film *Girl with Green Eyes* with her friend Rita Tushingham, star of *A Taste of Honey*. She had long worried about her weight, admitting to a tendency to get 'enormously fat', but now she was specifically told by director Silvio Narizzano not to diet as her character had to be big and awkward. She had a starring role opposite big names and she had a licence to *eat*:

The long hours made me very hungry and I ate non-stop, no guilt and no self-hatred. I was <u>following orders!</u>

There were press interviews during filming and Lynn was hurt to read headlines such as 'Ugly Duckling of the Redgrave Family'. She consoled herself with the rationalisation that it was because she had conducted the interviews wearing Georgy's baggy jumper (even though one journalist remarked 'Well, that's the way you usually dress, isn't it?'). As for the role itself, while Lynn felt she and Georgy were very different she could see there were parallels, including Georgy's awkwardness with her body and her sexuality. When she was overweight, Lynn would find the touch of a man's hands on the extra roll of fat on her waist almost unbearable, since it would give her a feeling of such self-loathing that romance always seemed out of the question. 'I sympathize with her...I used to have the same problems as her unattractiveness.'

She spent the first three weeks filming solely with suave James Mason, who was due to go abroad – falling a little in love with him and crying when he had to leave. She couldn't have had a better start than with James, Lynn would later say:

From the very first day on the set, he treated me as an equal, never patronizing, but always ready with advice and encouragement if you seemed to need it...James made me feel that if I tried I could do anything...and he told me always to close my eyes just before the camera started to roll. First because it would help to concentrate my mind on the scene, and second it would make my pupils look bigger and better. I've always remembered to do that.

James, for his part, was very enthusiastic about the quirkiness of the story and the chance it gave him to use his native Yorkshire accent. He was eager for the film to see the light of day and took little money for it. After he left, Lynn went on to shoot the rest of the film with the other co-stars. For a party scene she had to wear what she called 'this awful Shirley Bassey-type sequin dress' and sing *I'm a Whole Lot of Woman*, difficult for Lynn as she sang soprano well but struggled with that kind of 'Red Hot Mama' key, as she put it. The song had to be recorded beforehand and because of Lynn's extreme nervousness her voice emerged as small and squeaky rather than loud and sexy as demanded – an effect seemingly rectified for the final cut, when the song, and Lynn's vamp performance, is exactly right.

During shooting, the backers were nervous about the storyline and also worried that the combination of James Mason and two relative unknowns would not add up to much at the box office; production had been delayed several times when finances wobbled. Once the film was finished no one seemed to know what to do with it. Lynn and Alan Bates were invited to see a rough cut, without music and sound effects, at a preview for the director and

227

producers and executives from Columbia, and after the screening there was dead silence, not even a 'well done' to the actors. Lynn, in a state of shock about the lack of reaction, was taken for an Italian meal by Alan and they tried to convince themselves that the film would be better once the score was added. Alan at the time had his own troubles: during the making of *Georgy Girl* his Israeli dancer girlfriend, concerned about his bisexuality and previous relationships with men, had rejected his proposal of marriage.

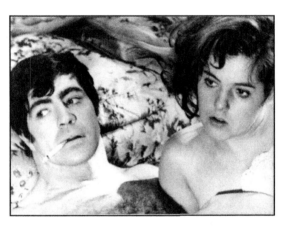

The film was made in black and white, for economy, and came out in 1966. It was rated X by the British Board of Film Censors, although reportedly coming close to being refused any classification at all, with its scandalous sex scenes and references to Meredith's multiple abortions. (The X was later reduced to an A, making it viewable by over-16s.) The screenplay keeps fairly closely to the novel, including its moralistic ending, although for some reason the director makes James Mason look suddenly chapfallen on realising he has taken on the baby as well as Georgy, when in the novel he heartily welcomes his new family. Because of much zany larking about, however – Alan Bates jumping over barriers and gradually shedding his clothing in supposed passion as he pursues Lynn through the streets – the film comes across as something quite different: a tale of Swinging London, akin to iconic 1960s films like *Alfie*, *Blow-Up* and *The Knack*. All three of the central characters play well – if Alan perhaps overdoing the quirkiness, Charlotte the bitchiness and Lynn the galumphing about – but of the three it is arguably Lynn who comes across as most convincing in the role.

The theme song was, unforgettably, *Georgy Girl* by the Australian group The Seekers, with its famous whistling intro. The music was by Tom Springfield, brother of Dusty, while the lyrics were rather surprisingly written by *Carry On* actor Jim Dale. He was rumoured to have been paid £20,000 – far more than Margaret for her story in the first place, if so, but the piece did get nominated for both a Golden Globe Award for Best Original Song and an Academy Award for Best Original Song. (The Seekers were unable to perform at the Academy Awards ceremony because at the time they were contractually bound to remain in Britain playing at a pantomime.) The song had been a fairly late appendage to the film, which was already completed when a question arose about the music that was playing over the titles in the opening sequence. The film's producer wanted the Seekers to be the ones to sing, and invited the group to a private screening to see if they were interested. Lead singer Judith Durham loved the film and was happy with their manager's decision to let the group replace the existing opener – 'a very Frank Sinatra-sounding, crooning song', she remembered. Tom Springfield was commissioned to write the tune and a classic was born – in one critic's words, 'the perfect pop song'.

Lynn Redgrave and director Silvio Narizzano went to see the Seekers perform in their turn and Lynn agreed that Judith, with her 'clear, warm clarion call of a voice', was the perfect choice to introduce Georgy to audiences. She also felt that while the Seekers were wonderful as a group, it was Judith who had held her attention – recognising that perhaps she saw herself in the singer. They were the same age, and now, in 'those strange heady days in the Sixties when we were young and all things seemed possible', she began to experience a sense of kinship. *Georgy Girl* changed her life, Lynn later acknowledged, and she always knew that much of it was down to the title song and Judith in particular. In 1997 she sent a screened message for Judith's Australian *This Is Your Life* episode, saying she believed the song was so integral to the success of the film because Judith's glorious voice embodied the spirit that she was trying to project on screen. Her own launch and success thirty years previously were down to Judith, she declared.

Judith experienced a similar sense of kinship with Lynn. When *Georgy Girl* was privately screened for the Seekers to help them decide about getting involved, the film immediately touched a nerve. She was shaken by how closely she identified with the main character. Judith was then in her early twenties and, in the early days of her success, still making her own dresses for performances.

She was self-conscious about the fact that (in her eyes) she was overweight, not pretty, and did not measure up to stardom:

It was the story of my life...I couldn't believe it. I related so strongly to Lynn Redgrave's role, and wished I could have played it. In the opening scene she's been to a hairdresser and is so unhappy with the way they've tried to make her look that she runs into a subway bathroom and washes it out under a tap. That scene was just me to a T! I'd been to a hairdresser especially for my appearances that first time on 'In Melbourne Tonight' back in 1963 and they did this awful beehive and I clearly remember wanting to put my head under a tap and wash it all out...

As regards the song itself Judith came out with contradictory statements over the years: that she liked it, and that the lyrics about loneliness and longing for love mirrored her own feelings at the time, but also that it did nothing for her emotionally and she never understood why people loved it so much. She admitted that it was actually quite difficult to sing because of the huge range, and that she had had to enlist one of the male band members to sing along with her on the lower notes. With the words slightly altered, the song eventually reached number one in the Seekers' home country, number one on a US chart – displacing the Monkees' *I'm a Believer* – number three in the UK, and sold over 11 million copies worldwide. (Rumour has it that the film's director had originally deemed it a hopeless 'tack on' to what he intended to be a serious farce.)

Georgy Girl the movie was a huge success, both at home and internationally, and was shortlisted for four Academy Awards and four Bafta prizes. Costing just $400,000 to make, by 1969 it had earned an estimated $7 million in the US alone and $6 million elsewhere. (Co-scriptwriter and respected playwright Peter Nichols, despite his disparaging remarks about the film, acknowledged it made 'a zillion dollars' and also that it was the only work he was known by in much of America.) Lynn won a Golden Globe and was judged best actress by New York film critics, while Alan was nominated by the Hollywood Foreign Press Association for best actor and most promising newcomer. American independent film importers and distributors eventually judged *Georgy Girl* best foreign film in English of the year and Lynn the best foreign actress. There were yet more prizes, including from the Office Catholique International du Cinéma, doubtless for the film's implicit moral message that the rightful place for bringing up children is within the sanctity of marriage. Lynn appeared, with her sister Vanessa, on the cover of *Time* magazine in March 1967.

British critics were not always so thrilled. 'Another swinging London story filled with people running through London late at night, dancing madly in the rain, and visiting deserted children's playgrounds to ride on the roundabouts,' carped the British Film Institute. A rather poor imitation of new wave filmmaking, their review continued, with a slick line in amusing but shallow repartee which soon palled, as did the repeated jokes about the heroine's size (Jos calls Georgy 'fat face' all the way through the film – as opposed to only once in the novel – and Meredith, as she did in the book, tells her she is built like the back of a bus). The film's structure was jerky, jumping from scene to scene and relying on continuous snatches of loud music for linkage. 'The potentially excellent cast and the promising comedienne talent of Lynn Redgrave can do little in the face of such opposition from both script and direction,' was the damning conclusion. Georgy was the sort of girl that every young man dreaded being saddled with on a blind date, said the *Daily Mirror*, although going on to find her one of the most touching heroines of the year and the film itself 'shining bright, gay, and thoroughly enjoyable'. For dramatist Peter Ustinov, Lynn gave the impression of 'knocking things down by mistake because she doesn't know her tail is wagging'. An inconsiderable and improbable plot redeemed by the acting of the three main characters, judged the *Illustrated London News*.

As for any message in the film, for some critics it was merely an enjoyably quirky comedy, with Alan Bates 'splendid' as the 'brazen and bumptious mod lover'. Others, seemingly more tuned in to Margaret Forster's own thinking, saw in Meredith and Jos' behaviour a serious indictment of irresponsibility and immaturity in the younger generation and the ending as a complete rejection of 1960s values. The Catholic Church agreed, declaring that while the film did illustrate promiscuity at its absolute worst, its heroine nevertheless aspired to home and hearth.

For the public, *Georgy Girl* in 1966 quite simply captured the feeling of the decade (even if, as later noted by renowned film critic Alexander Walker, it just missed being able to include references to the newly emerging drug scene). People flocked to see it, though generally finding the character of Jos hard to understand or really like and Georgy's decision to marry the older, ponderous James – even for the sake of the baby – a surprising one. Some viewers just enjoyed the show, oblivious to any messages or nuances of character: a female fan approached Alan at a press conference to gush about the artistry with which he had removed his clothes. 'After years of learning my craft,' Alan commented drily, 'I get compliments for my ability to take off my pants in public.'

Abroad, the *Canberra Times* – groaning that Australia was sick of kitchen sink cinema imported from the motherland – saw *Georgy Girl* as a sentimental and mistakenly unrealistic seasoning of sugar-daddy fantasy worked into the usual recipe of working-class sexuality in drizzly old Britain. James Mason was 'pouchy' and Lynn Redgrave very good, but it was lively and virile Alan Bates who was responsible for much of the real comedy in the film, the review decided. Across the Atlantic, where Margaret's novel was published that same year, filmgoers and critics alike were enthusiastic. Lynn played 'one of those big bony English broads usually associated with horses and tweeds', observed the Canadian magazine *Maclean's*, and the film was from the life's-a-giggle school of comedy with Lynn larking about non-stop, but doing so with 'looks, talent, energy, and charm'. 'Would you like to have an orgy with Georgy?' blared the posters in the

US, along with lines such as 'the wildest thing to hit the world since the miniskirt'. Reviewers loved it, although clearly astonished by a less than perfect heroine. The review in *Life* magazine noted Lynn's bad hair and terrible clothes and described her as an ugly duckling searching for love, but still 'an irresistible girl, funny and alive'. The film was both hilarious and moving, observed the critic, the kind of comedy which the English seemed to do better than Americans because they were less afraid of mixing fun with genuine emotion. The characters did nutty things but stopped this side of absurdity, and their universally human predicament was 'slyly but compassionately revealed'. The character of Meredith, though, was dismissed as so bitchy as to be unbelievable, and one of the few flaws in the film.

§

The *New York Times* had been particularly withering about Lynn's personal appearance. 'Treetop tall (5' 10"),' said the review, 'and all kneecaps, with hair that never seems to have met a stylist, a little round mouth invented for devouring hot fudge sundaes and a chubby figure that changes weight according to her mood, she certainly doesn't look like a star.'

Lynn understood how 'fantastically fortunate' she had been to get the role but these comments must have hurt. After finishing the film she went to what she called a fat farm to starve off the extra pounds gained during its making, accompanied for moral support by her old friend Rita Tushingham.

She was eventually sent to the Berlin Film Festival to help with promotion, which involved making an appearance after a showing of the film. Staring up at the 'distorted, twisted, massive' figure on screen as she waited in the wings, Lynn felt sick, knowing that she was seeing herself as others saw her. The pounds had crept back on, and when she was offered more fat girl parts she turned to extreme dieting to lose weight and later became a spokesperson for Weight Watchers. She married actor John Clark in 1967 (serenaded at their wedding feast with the strains of *Georgy Girl* played on piano and violin), had three children, and enjoyed a long and successful acting career. In 2002 she received an OBE for services to acting. She died of breast cancer in 2010, aged sixty-seven.

Regarding the role she had played in *Georgy Girl*, Lynn actually thought there was more to Georgy than people imagined and also that the story had a 'very dark almost sick side to it'. She saw the character perhaps more truly as Margaret Forster had created her, not as pathetic, but

> *...very ruthless. Most people saw her as a sweet softy. I don't think she was a softy at all. She was manipulating and very shrewd. People loved her, I think, because they recognized their own terrible faults, and were glad to see them put up on the screen.*

As for her co-stars, Charlotte Rampling, only eighteen when offered the part, revealed much later in life that she all but abandoned British cinema after *Georgy Girl* for fear of having to play another bitch role like Meredith. She still thought it was a fantastic film, learning as she went along in a rather improvised way by watching other people, which at the time she thought 'very cool'. After the film came out she was told that Meredith was so unlikeable she would never work again – that she had played the part so convincingly, people would assume she must be like the character. Alan Bates disliked his role too, for different reasons. He saw Jos – the film version – as unable to dispense with his own pleasures in order to take on responsibility: 'I didn't think he was funny. I felt he was an infinitely sad character, and I found him easy to play, because he's a bit like me – a person escaping into a fantasy world...He was really a bit past behaving like a kid – he needed to grow up, but there was nothing underneath the fun and games'.

Many years later Judith Durham of The Seekers went to visit Lynn backstage after seeing her one-woman show *Shakespeare for My Father* at the Melbourne International Festival of 1994. Lynn was delighted:

After the performance, there she was, in my dressing room. My singing alter ego. Her appearance unchanged by the years. With what joy we embraced. Life can be so strangely magical. Two older women, not girls any more but feeling like girls at that moment. Meeting again, reaching out across the years and recognising what they have both meant to each other.

§

Margaret did not attend the world premiere of the film in the West End in July 1966 (or, as far as is known, the Broadway musical version *Georgy!* in 1970, which flopped – hampered by being unable to use the famous Seekers song in the show). But with the success of the film the novel was reissued in paperback with the stars of the film on the cover, and sales rose steeply. Suddenly, even after the success of the original novel, Margaret Forster was a name.

After the triumph of *Georgy Girl*, book and film, she settled into a long lifetime of writing (with 'Author of *Georgy Girl*' on the cover of her next effort), as did Hunter, by then gaining increasing visibility as a journalist and as the first serious biographer of the Beatles. When Hunter became anxious to return some of the hospitality he had enjoyed from the group he invited each of them home to meet the family. The unmusical Margaret was not particularly keen to meet them, and downright refused to invite friends over at the same time as that would have been showing off. Paul and his then girlfriend Jane Asher came for tea and played happily with the children, while George on his visit with his first wife Pattie Boyd was more intent on having a philosophical discussion. For vegetarian Ringo and his first wife Maureen, Margaret went to a great deal of trouble concocting a meal out of aubergines only to discover that the only vegetable Ringo actually liked was potatoes. Luckily she had made several puddings, which then became the entire meal.

Looking back, Margaret was never proud of *Georgy Girl*. It was not really the novel she had had in mind, and it became 'like an albatross around my neck', a flippant work that had sent her off down the wrong track. But one thing Margaret was clear about – she was not Georgy:

People have great fun pretending I must either be Meredith or Georgy and I can tell who likes me by their choice. The silly thing is that I go to such an effort to get inside the characters. I strain towards objectivity and loathe any suggestion of myself in it.

She was grateful that it had truly got her started and that with the film came money: her career had been launched with 'incredible ease'. By the 1990s Margaret professed to be 'filled with grief' that *Georgy Girl*, the novel she had written all those years ago in her twenties, was still in print. It was almost as though she had done nothing since. In fact, she stated, it took her eight more novels and ten years to get herself on the road that she should have been on all along – probably meaning the writing of books about women's role in the family and society and about contemporary family relationships, often against a backdrop of clashing class values as children grow away from their roots. One character Margaret returned to more than a few times: as in *Georgy Girl*, a rebellious, unconventional daughter at odds with her parents – particularly the remote father, whom she treats with hatred or contempt.

When her three children started arriving Margaret found herself better able to understand her own mother, who had given up a beloved office job in local government to get married and have a family (although in truth she had had no choice: at that time married women were not allowed to work for the government). Margaret's solution to the career-or-children dilemma was simple: by choosing writing she could have both, easily fitting in her work around the demands of home and family with Hunter's help. There was no question of employing a cleaner, however. Margaret hated the idea of telling some other woman, who might be the age of her mother, to clean or dust. She enjoyed being a mother and looking after Hunter and was not even averse to doing housework, 'a real Northern working-class feeling' (although admitting that getting through all the domestic jobs each day as efficiently as possible was actually a scheme to secure time for herself at the end of it). The house had to be gleaming, and also beautiful, as perhaps programmed into her by her hardworking parent. She did not regard her writing as a job. It was just play to Margaret, said Hunter: her children came first. Had she been forced to choose between a career and motherhood, Margaret would have made the same decision as her mother:

...I was, when it came to the crunch, exactly like my mother and grandmother; family first, no argument.

When writing a biography of author Daphne du Maurier, she said that she admired her subject except for her behaviour as a mother, which to Margaret was 'deeply shocking', in that Daphne totally favoured her son over her daughters and put her writing before her children, taking little interest in their well-being – even as regards providing them with food. Perhaps, she said doubtfully, it made Daphne the more dedicated writer.

She was no strident and angry feminist, therefore, and was frank that she might not have had the nerve to be a suffragette or would ever go marching. 'Too fond of home.' Her early rage against the lot of women, and her burning drive to escape it, had gradually given way to a love of family and a sense of the importance of domestic life. But she was acutely conscious of how lucky she had been to have it all, and how her life as a woman had differed from that of her working-class forebears. In 1983 she published *Significant Sisters: The Grassroots of Active Feminism 1839 – 1939,* a work of non-fiction tracing the lives of eight famous women who had brought about vital changes in spheres such as education, medicine and the law. And despite owning up to being a 'feeble feminist', her final choice on *Desert Island Discs* in 1994 was *March of the Women,* Ethel Smyth's choral work in celebration of the suffragettes.

Margaret was always a prickly person, with very decided opinions. 'She never quite liked things, or didn't care, or didn't know, or was not bothered,' said Hunter. According to Hunter his wife was a true Cumbrian, her ingrained character inherited from her Cumbrian father. As such she was intensely private. Her pride did not allow her to reveal weaknesses or worries; private and personal things she kept to herself, even from her husband. She was inherently pessimistic – this time inherited from her mother, she believed – always seeing the worst ahead and imagining herself to a point where something awful happened. If it did happen, this put her in a better position to cope. But at the same time she had wit, and could be funny in real life and in letters (if less so in her books), and also a true friend. People confided in her.

Margaret continued to write until her death, her subject always women. She produced a hugely popular array of novels, biography and memoir – including *Precious Lives* in 1998, in which she picked apart her tempestuous relationship with her by now dead father. As an adult she had naturally begun to feel a sense of duty towards him as he aged, and also gratitude, if not love. She increasingly came to sense a bond with him, the tie of blood, and indeed respect for the unyielding strength of character with which she had struggled in her youth. He died at the age of ninety-six, leaving Margaret in a state of surprising sadness and regret for the man she had had such contempt for. Her mother was always easier to understand, her choice of 'home and family first' the same as Margaret's own, so that ultimately she came to see how much they had in common.

Her books brought her great joy in their writing, which she described as 'a bit like chatting to myself', and brought too the material wealth she had set her sights on as a teenager to escape her origins. Some of this she gave away, particularly early on, when she and Hunter were young and healthy and had enough for their own needs. She bought her parents a bungalow and put at least one of her book contracts in the name of a charity, which then received all the royalties. But Margaret never undervalued money, and sensibly scoffed at those who did. Money, she said, '...brings you *enormous* happiness!' When newly rich from their literary efforts she and Hunter and the children had enjoyed a sabbatical year in Malta and Portugal, and they later bought a much loved second home for summers in the Lake District.

In 1975 Margaret was elected a Fellow of the Royal Society of Literature and in subsequent years became the recipient of a whole swathe of awards for non-fiction: the Heinemann Award of the Royal Society of Literature in 1989, the Writers' Guild Award for Best Non-Fiction in 1993, the Fawcett Society Book Prize in 1994, the Lex Prize of The Global Business Book Award in 1998 and the J. R. Ackerley Prize for Autobiography in 1999. But she never took herself too seriously as a writer, keeping her distance from literary circles and eschewing self-promotion. In her early years of being published she did do some TV and radio and signing sessions, and appeared at a few literary festivals, but never with pleasure because she felt it catered to her worst instincts. She disliked that part of herself that performed and came out with glib and instant opinions. It was not an author's duty to appear in public, Margaret ultimately decided. She preferred to be at home, or, if out at the theatre or cinema, to sit entirely alone: 'I am antisocial. I am not gregarious. I do like to be on my own.' She only grudgingly agreed to go with a friend to see Lynn Redgrave in her *Shakespeare for My Father* show in London in the 1990s, but, unlike Judith Durham, refused to go backstage although Lynn would have been thrilled to see her. For Margaret such a step would have been pushy and gushing. She even turned down Prime Minister Tony Blair's invitation to Downing Street for his notorious 1997 victory party, despite her lifelong commitment to Labour (as a 'lazy, lazy member').

Notwithstanding such antisocial inclinations she was always very curious about other people, liking to sit in buses 'eavesdropping like mad' and speculating about those around her, even if not actually wanting to meet them. She loved to read and review new fiction and was fascinated by Margaret Drabble, as they had published their first novels within a year of each other and had been at their respective universities at the same time. Although not much in contact, she used to say that if rung up for her views on writing then a similar call had just gone, or was about to go, to the other Margaret.

She died from cancer in 2016, happily free from pain towards the end and able to read, without which she said there would be nothing to live for.

In every obituary she was 'Margaret Forster, author of *Georgy Girl*'.

Afterword

Were these writers 'Angry Young Women'? Anger can certainly be discerned in some of their works: in *A Taste of Honey*, *Up the Junction*, and *Poor Cow*, the characters are angry about the treatment of women and about their hard lives in the lower reaches of society. Penelope Mortimer's *The Pumpkin Eater* was written in a different sort of anger, the white-hot fury of a woman betrayed. But Shelagh Delaney hated the 'Angry Young Woman' label and insisted her play was more about resilience in the face of adversity. What have I got to be angry about? she asked. Lynne Reid Banks felt the same, deliberately distancing herself from the male group and original 'Angry Young Man' John Osborne in particular, while for Margaret Drabble things 'hadn't yet reached the stage of being angry'. The 'Angry Young Woman' tag, it seems, was mostly repudiated. They were also never a group. A few knew each other and were friends; the rest did not, and some objected to being lumped together.

Were these writers, then, feminists in the making, as so often argued? They did raise, through the stories they told, the issues that at the time lay buried beneath the surface of female lives: lack of equal pay and opportunities, of free and accessible contraception, of choice about motherhood. Discussion arising from their works almost certainly informed the seismic societal changes that were about to come, with the pill made available for single women in 1967, followed by the 1967 Abortion Act and the 1970 Equal Pay Act. But for the most part these young women equivocated about their early feminist credentials. While Lynne Reid Banks subsequently argued that she had been an unconscious feminist when pioneering a new way of life as a woman reporter, others hedged: Nell Dunn felt that she had never written with a feminist agenda, Margaret Drabble wavered about the use of the term in relation to her younger self, and Margaret Forster owned up to being but a 'feeble feminist'.

Indeed, at the time they were writing, Lynne Reid Banks thought men the superior sex (even if changing her mind later), while Nell Dunn told the *Daily Mail* that the running of the country should be left to men and that for women love was always the paramount thing in life. As for the central characters in all of their works, they too evince little in the way of traditionally understood feminism. Far from railing against their lot, they bear injustice and inequality with no obvious sense of unfairness or resentment at patriarchal attitudes. Careers are mostly absent: Jane in *The L-Shaped Room* and Jo in *A Taste of Honey* both give up on work because of pregnancy – apparently with little regret – while the women in Nell Dunn's novels either have temporary menial jobs or are housewives, and Mrs Armitage in *The Pumpkin Eater* has seemingly never worked at all. There is no sisterhood: pregnant, unmarried Jo in *A Taste of Honey* gets support only from her male friend Geof, and for the most part the rest of the fictional women suffer and deal with their problems alone. Some indeed positively reject the idea of female solidarity: *Poor Cow* Joy specifically states that she can't stand the constant company of 'bleeding women'. Equally, there is no attempt to break free of traditional attitudes to females – indeed the reverse. Some of these heroines have no complaints about being sex objects, and enjoy the feeling of being desired. The men Joy has had sex with may only have wanted her body, she admits, but 'well that is me – me body – what else do you expect them to like you for, yer three piece suite?'

What is certainly new is the frank need for sex, stated in a surprisingly open way for the time: Jane discovers it, Joy adores it, and Georgy is desperate for it. It's not true, says Georgy, that a woman has to be roused by someone before she has any sexual awakening:

I've felt it for years, in an absolute vacuum and it doesn't need anyone to rouse me. I'm just ripe for plucking...I used to get myself into an absolute passion when I was about twelve imagining myself stripping in front of men. I just couldn't wait for sex. I still can't.

Georgy Girl, Margaret Forster, 1965

But what is most striking is the supreme importance to these writers of having children.

Margaret Drabble and Margaret Forster each specifically stated that their novels were about motherhood, and both of their heroines are besotted with their babies, Georgy even resenting the previously loved Jos as an interruption in her relationship with little Sara. Jane in *The L-Shaped Room*, after fearing a miscarriage, feels 'a tremor that was partly apprehension and partly excitement. Still in there, safe and growing!' Mrs Armitage rages because she has been robbed of her pregnancy and any future hope of one, while for Joy in *Poor Cow* looking after her beloved Jonny is sheer pleasure, and she longs for another child to enjoy:

I can't stop looking into prams. I can't stop thinking about a little girl...She's going to have everything – the lot, one of them Spanish layettes all lace. Lace around her little hands and a handmade shawl to wrap her in and one of them cradles in pink organdie...

Poor Cow, Nell Dunn, 1967

And she loves being pregnant: 'I want a white dress with a great big black bow to go over me lump – it'll look terrific with me blonde hair.' The role of mother, far from being resented, offers delight, consolation and self-worth. Although conflicted about her imminent motherhood, Jo in *A Taste of Honey* declares: 'Do you know, for the first time in my life I feel really important. I feel as though I could take care of the whole world.' Tellingly, it is only the repellent Meredith in *Georgy Girl* who feels nothing for children, dismissing her newborn as hideous and calling for it to be adopted.

So important is motherhood to these fictional characters (and indeed having a choice in the matter – abortion in most of these works is either considered, attempted, rejected or actually undergone) that when they accidentally get pregnant, Jane, Rosamund, and Jo all make the unheard-of decision to keep their babies as single parents and go out to work to support them. Georgy, not herself a mother, opts to take on the baby of her friend and do the same thing. Men are superfluous to this decision – either dispensable or a necessary evil. In order to be with their children the women choose either to remain without partners or to compromise with someone inadequate: Georgy with the corpulent James, Mrs Armitage with unfaithful Jake, Joy with violent Tom. Margaret Forster said of Georgy that she wanted marriage 'but not necessarily a man, except as the means to the end'. Sex may be important to these characters, but it is motherhood that is paramount.

Margaret Forster's own trajectory through life was an interesting one – moving from youthful horror at the idea of promising to obey during the marriage ceremony, and a fervent desire to avoid the traps of marriage and family, to an awakening desire for children and a wholehearted commitment to the role of wife and mother. A wife in the twenty-first century was a much stronger creature, she still maintained, not at all submissive, and able to match her husband right for right – but she nevertheless viewed it as reasonable that Hunter's writing should take precedence over hers. He mostly earned a regular salary which paid the bills, she said, and she knew she would always put home and family first. In this respect, admitted Margaret, 'I am feeble.' She never asked that Hunter lose sleep in the night to a screaming baby, and did not resent it. Hunter was the breadwinner, and her job was motherhood.

Arguably, these six authors were neither angry nor feminists in the commonly understood interpretation of those words, but something else: young women writing of the deep significance of motherhood in their lives. Their contribution to feminism was incidental, and some openly regretted their lack of militancy. As encapsulated by Penelope Mortimer, what they had really written about was quite other:

...love (and sex and hate); and the creation of children.

The Pumpkin Eater, Penelope Mortimer, 1962

Read these works, and see the films: they are classics of their time, and they had something surprising to say.

If you enjoyed reading this book, I would love to hear what you think. Please leave a review on Amazon.

Thank you.

Also by Anne Wellman:

A Life of Anne Tyler

Anne Tyler has been acknowledged as one of America's greatest living novelists. An inspiring chronicler of what lies beneath the everyday, she has written twenty-four acclaimed works, her first in 1964 when she was just twenty-three, and her most recent at the age of eighty. Her best-known novels include *Dinner at the Homesick Restaurant* and *The Accidental Tourist*, made into an Oscar-winning movie. She is greatly loved by her legions of fans all around the world.

But for decades, Anne avoided all public appearances and publicity, refusing to talk about herself or her life. Now, for the first time, this gripping biography unveils all— from Anne's childhood in a Quaker commune to her astonishing writing career and happy years in Baltimore, the city ever present in her work and almost a character in itself. Her story reveals the many experiences and preoccupations that were reflected in her writing and Anne emerges as a woman with great charm, warmth, and humor —but one far bleaker in her estimation of the human race than might ever be guessed.

Available from:

In the UK: https://www.amazon.co.uk/Life-Anne-Tyler-Wellman-ebook/dp/B0B8F2GS69

In the US: https://www.amazon.com/Life-Anne-Tyler-Wellman/dp/B0B8H967J3

Also available in other Amazon markets

Also by Anne Wellman:

BETTY

The Story of Betty MacDonald, Author of *The Egg and I*

In 1945 Betty MacDonald published *The Egg and I*, a lightly fictionalised account of her life as the wife of a chicken farmer in the remote American Northwest in the 1920s. The book was an immediate success, selling a million copies in less than a year, and was eventually translated into over thirty languages. A Hollywood movie of the book appeared two years later and at least eight further movies based on the popular *Egg and I* characters Ma and Pa Kettle were to follow.

In the decade following, Betty wrote a number of highly popular children's books (*Mrs Piggle-Wiggle* being the best known) and three more semi-autobiographical works. Her four comic memoirs of a life in the West and Northwest range from a rough mining community in Montana to the lush Olympic Peninsula and the bright lights of big city Seattle, and her life may even be viewed as a paradigm of early twentieth-century American experience: pioneering, homesteading, the Great Depression, war, and finally prosperity.

This is Betty's true story.

Available from:

In the UK: https://www.amazon.co.uk/dp/1493662422

In the US: https://www.amazon.com/dp/1493662422

Also available in other Amazon markets

Also by Anne Wellman:

MONICA

A Life of Monica Dickens

'All I have ever done is to report the experiences of my life.'

So said Charles Dickens' great-granddaughter Monica Dickens, author of twenty-five novels and many classics for children, and one of the most popular writers of her day. Born into the upper classes, as a bored and unhappy debutante in the 1930s she took the incredible step of going into domestic service. *One Pair of Hands*, the book Monica wrote about her exploits, sold in the millions and has never been out of print since. Her subsequent works, calling on her rich experience as a wartime nurse, Spitfire factory worker, GI bride and more, sold in similar numbers but are now largely forgotten.

Often dismissed as a 'light' writer, and her widespread appeal deflecting serious recognition, Monica Dickens was nevertheless highly praised by some of the most respected authors of the twentieth century, and indeed beyond. Far from writing lightly, in her middle period she addressed issues such as child abuse, suicide, and inner city deprivation. Her novels, always threaded with humour, were immensely understanding of human frailties, but at the same time urged resilience and responsibility for one's fellow man. These were qualities that Monica herself possessed in plenty. After becoming a volunteer for the Samaritans in England, this deeply compassionate woman went on to found the first branch of the organization in America and hence to save countless lives. Her name is engraved on a marker near the soaring bridges over the Cape Cod canal, where she campaigned for the erection of higher barriers to stop desperate people jumping to their deaths.

In her early sixties Monica produced an account of the experiences in her life which had influenced her writing, her 1978 memoir *An Open Book*. 'This is not the whole story of a life,' begins the first chapter, and in truth much was omitted or by her own admission confused with the semi-autobiographical works she had written as a young woman. *An Open Book* is a valuable starting-point but this first biography seeks to fill the gaps and to tell the story of her later years, with the help of contemporary accounts, family histories, interviews with close friends, personal articles and private correspondence, and not least Monica's major works and their critical reception.

All her writing life Monica was compared to Charles Dickens, not always favourably. And yet the similarities between them are there: eccentric characters, humorous observation of the English scene, social conscience, an optimistic and moral view of life – but above all, talent for the written word.

Available from:

In the UK:

   https://www.amazon.co.uk/dp/B07HLM73WS

In the US:

   https://www.amazon.com/dp/B07HLM73WS

Also available in other Amazon markets

Bibliography

A Taste of Honey: Shelagh Delaney

A Taste of Honey, film, 1961

Bryan, Dora, *According to Dora*, Hodder and Stoughton, 1987

Cooke, Rachel, *Shelagh Delaney: the return of Britain's angry young woman*, The Observer, 2014

Coren, Michael, *Theatre Royal: 100 Years of Stratford East*, Quartet Books, 1984

Daily Mail, 1 January 1961

Delaney, Shelagh, *A Taste of Honey*, original script, British Library (https://www.bl.uk/collection-items/manuscript-of-a-taste-of-honey-by-shelagh-delaney)

Delaney, Shelagh, *Sweetly Sings the Donkey*, Penguin, 1968

Delaney, Shelagh, *Shelagh Delaney's Salford*, BBC, a Ken Russell film for *Monitor*, 1960

De Jongh, Nicholas, *The Guardian*, 25 November 2011

Goddard, Simon, *Mozipedia, the Encyclopaedia of Morrissey and the Smiths*, Ebury Press, 2012

Harding, John, *Sweetly Sings Delaney*, Greenwich Exchange, London, 2014

https://www.youtube.com/watch?v=Yr9u-dc_EKg&t=38s
https://www.youtube.com/watch?v=iYT0iLVmjiA
https://youtube.com/watch?v=SM22loR53TQ
https://www.theoldie.co.uk/blog/still-with-us-rita-tushingham

https://www.salixhomes.org/news/artist-harold-riley-unveils-shelagh-delaney-plaque

https://sounds.bl.uk/Arts-literature-and-performance/Theatre-Archive-Project/024M-C1142X000225-0100V0

https://www.bl.uk/collection-items/letters-between-shelagh-delaney-gerry-raffles-and-the-arts-council-1958

https://www.bl.uk/20th-century-literature/videos/breaking-barriers-murray-melvin-on-a-taste-of-honey

https://www.bbc.co.uk/sounds/play/b017clx3

https://www.bbc.co.uk/news/entertainment-arts-43626593

http://ritatushingham.com/

https://www.telegraph.co.uk/news/obituaries/culture-obituaries/theatre-obituaries/8905444/Shelagh-Delaney.html

https://www.theguardian.com/books/2010/sep/18/jeanette-winterson-my-hero-shelagh-delaney

https://www.theguardian.com/stage/2003/sep/10/theatre2

https://www.youtube.com/watch?v=T8opucP3PRo&t=31s

https://www.theguardian.com/culture/2018/apr/10/how-we-made-a-taste-of-honey-rita-tushingham

https://www.theguardian.com/stage/2011/nov/25/taste-of-honey-gay-ban

https://www.theguardian.com/stage/2014/jan/25/shelagh-delaney-angry-young-woman-a-taste-of-honey

https://www.youtube.com/watch?v=T8opucP3PRo

https://www.youtube.com/watch?v=SM22loR53TQ

https://louisewoodwardstyles.wixsite.com/shelaghdelaneyday

https://www.criterion.com/current/posts/4192-morrissey-s-taste-for-shelagh-delaney

http://www.screenonline.org.uk/tv/id/1284964/index.html

http://www.salfordstar.com/article.asp?id=3910

Lewenstein, Oscar, *Kicking against the pricks : a theatre producer looks back : the memoirs of Oscar Lewenstein*, Nick Hern Books, 1994

Littlewood, Joan, *Joan's Book: Joan Littlewood's Peculiar History As She Tells It*, Methuen, 2003

Muller, Robert, *The Lucretia Borgia of Salford Lancs*, Daily Mail, 9 February 1959

Nye, Louise Kimpton, *Looking at the original script for A Taste of Honey*, 7 September 2017, British Library

Patton, Alec, *Jazz and Music-Hall Transgressions in Theatre Workshop's Production of A Taste of Honey*, (https://www.cambridge.org/core/journals/new-theatre-quarterly/article/jazz-and-musichall-transgressions-in-theatre-workshops-production-of-a-taste-of-honey/C983C8FFFEBEC4A3134BE7BFE642BFA0)

Salford City Reporter, 1958 – 59

Smith, James, *British Writers and MI5 Surveillance, 1930 – 1960*, Cambridge University Press, 2013

Taylor, John Russell, *The Angry Theatre: New British Drama*, Hill and Wang, 1969

Times, The, *A Taste of Honey*, film review, 13 September 1961

Todd, Selina, *Tastes of Honey*, Chatto & Windus, 2019

Tushingham, Rita, interview with Robert Ross, Renown Festival of Film, 2018

Welsh, James M, and Tibbetts, John C, *The Cinema of Tony Richardson: Essays and Interviews*, State University of New York Press, 1999

Winterson, Jeanette, *Shelagh Delaney: The Start of the Possible*, 7 September 2017, British Library

The L-Shaped Room: Lynne Reid Banks

Attenborough, Richard, and Diana Hawkins, *Richard Attenborough, Entirely Up to You, Darling*, Hutchinson, 2008

Banks, Lynne Reid, biography (https://biography.jrank.org/pages/1956/Reid-Banks-Lynne-1929.html)

Banks, Lynne Reid (http://www.lynnereidbanks.com/interview.html)

Banks, Lynne Reid, interview with writer and biographer Andrew Whitehead, 20 April 2000

Banks, Lynne Reid, interview with James Naughtie, *Bookclub*, Radio 4, 10 June 2010

Banks, Lynne Reid, interview with Jonathan Derbyshire, New Statesman, 10 September 2010

Banks, Lynne Reid, interview with Val Ross, Globe & Mail (Toronto, Canada), 26 October 1996

Banks, Lynne Reid, *Lynne Reid Banks: raising a family on a kibbutz was everything my mother detested*, The Guardian, 11 March 2017

Banks, Lynne Reid, obituary for husband Chaim Stephenson, The Guardian, 28 March 2016

Banks, Lynne Reid, *The Backward Shadow*, Vintage Classics, 2010

Banks, Lynne Reid, *The L-Shaped Room*, Vintage Digital, 2014

Banks, Lynne Reid, *Two is Lonely*, Vintage Classics, 2010

Banks, Lynne Reid, interview with Stephanie Nettell, *Books for Keeps*, March 1991 (http://booksforkeeps.co.uk/issue/67/childrens-books/articles/authorgraph/authorgraph-no67-lynne-reid-banks)

Briganti, Chiara, with Kathy Mezei, *Living With Strangers: Bedsits and Boarding Houses in Modern English Life, Literature and Film*, Bloomsbury Academic, 2018

Brown, Len, *Meetings with Morrissey*, Omnibus Press, April 2010

Caron, Leslie, BFI interview with Sue Harris, 23 August 2015

Caron, Leslie, *Thank Heaven...*, Plume Books, 2010

Cartwright, Alistair, *Life Between Walls: Race, Subdivision and Lodging Houses in Postwar London*, Architectural Histories, 8(1): 4, pp. 1–16. DOI: https://doi.org/10.5334/ah.378 2020

Forbes, Bryan, *A Divided Life*, Mandarin Paperbacks, 1993

Heilpern, John, *JOHN OSBORNE: A Patriot For Us*, Chatto and Windus, 2006

https://www.dailymotion.com/video/x72d63w (Leslie Caron)

https://www.theguardian.com/tv-and-radio/2011/aug/14/tv-news-50s-the-hour

https://www.londonfictions.com/lynne-reid-banks-the-l-shaped-room.html

https://www.newstatesman.com/books/2010/09/shaped-room-jane-novel-women

https://www.newstatesman.com/books/2010/09/interview-israel-writing-write

https://www.bbc.co.uk/programmes/b00sl3y1

http://www.screenonline.org.uk/media/mfb/973282/index.html

http://www.screenonline.org.uk/film/id/440753/index.html

https://www.theguardian.com/artanddesign/2016/mar/28/chaim-stephenson-obituary

Independent on Sunday, *The L-Shaped Room*, review, 26 September 2010

Morrissey, *never turn your back on mother earth*, Blitz magazine, May 1985 (interview with Patricia Phoenix)

Osborne, John, *A Better Class of Person*, Faber and Faber, 1992

The L-Shaped Room, film, 1962

Times, The, *Dear Sir or Madam* (on Paul McCartney), Barry Miles, 12 April 2008

Times Literary Supplement, *The L-Shaped Room*, review, 18 November 1960

Times Literary Supplement, *The L-Shaped Room*, film review, 16 November 1962

Whitebrook, Peter, *John Osborne 'Anger is not about...'* Oberon Books Ltd, 2015

The Pumpkin Eater: Penelope Mortimer

Bancroft, Anne, memorial booklet accompanying Jack Clayton retrospective, Washington DC, 1995

Cooke, Rachel, *Penelope Mortimer – return of the original angry young woman*, Guardian, June 2015 (https://www.theguardian.com/books/2015/jun/28/penelope-mortimer-the-pumpkin-eater-angry-young-woman)

Daniel, Douglass K, *Anne Bancroft: A Life*, University Press of Kentucky, 2017

Dundy, Elaine, *Finch, Bloody Finch*, Michael Joseph Ltd, 1980

Grove, Valerie, *A Voyage Round John Mortimer*, Penguin Group, 2007

Klein, Joanne, *Making Pictures: Pinter Screenplays*, Ohio State University Press, 1985

https://www.bbc.co.uk/programmes/b063zt9w

https://hitchensblog.mailonsunday.co.uk/2016/05/horace
-rumpole-john-mortimer-and-the-presumption-of-
innocence.html

https://www.nybooks.com/daily/2018/12/02/penelope-
mortimer-a-writing-life/

http://www.screenonline.org.uk/film/id/478062/index.ht
ml

https://www.imdb.com/title/tt0058500/

https://www.nytimes.com/1964/11/10/archives/screen-
the-pumpkin-eater-arrives-film-written-by-pinter-stars-
anne.html

Mortimer, Penelope, *The Pumpkin Eater*, Penguin, July 2015

Mortimer, Penelope, *About Time*, Penguin, 1979

Mortimer, Penelope, *About Time Too*, Phoenix, 1994

Scholes, Lucy, *Penelope Mortimer: A Writing Life*, The New York Review of Books, December 2018

Scholes, Lucy, *Re-covered: Saturday Lunch with the Brownings*, Paris Review, 17 April 2019
(https://www.theparisreview.org/blog/2019/04/17/re-
visited-saturday-lunch-with-the-brownings/)

Sinyard, Neil, *Jack Clayton*, Manchester University Press, 2000

The Pumpkin Eater, film, 1964

Poor Cow and Up the Junction: Nell Dunn

Anarchy Magazine, January 1964

Bell, Julia, and Paul Magrs, *The Creative Writing Coursebook: Forty-Four Authors Share Advice and Exercises for Fiction and Poetry*, Macmillan, 2019

Coatman, Anna, *Ways of listening* (https://unbound.com/boundless/2019/12/12/talking-about-womens-lives)

Cooke, Lez, *British Television Drama: A History*, British Film Institute, 2003

Daily Telegraph, Jeremy Sandford obituary, 14 May 2003

Davies, Hunter *Hunting People: Thirty Years of Interviews with the Famous*, Mainstream Publishing Company, 1994

Drabble, Margaret, Introduction to *Poor Cow*, 1987

Dunn, Nell, *International Herald Tribune* interview, 2 November 1996

Dunn, Nell, interview with British Theatre Guide London editor Philip Fisher, 23 July 2016

Dunn, Nell, *Poor Cow*, Virago, 2013

Dunn, Nell, Preface to *Poor Cow*, Virago, 2013

Dunn, Nell, Preface to *Up the Junction*, 1996

Dunn, Nell, *Up the Junction*, Virago, 2013

Dunn, Nell, *Talking to Women*, Preface and Afterword, Silver Press, May 2018

Dunn, Nell, *The Muse, A memoir of love at first sight*, Coronet, 2020

Dunn, Nell, *The Film Programme*, Radio 4, 26 June 2016

Garnett, Tony, *The Day the Music Died*, Constable, 2016

Garnett, Tony, writing about *Up the Junction*, Radio Times, 28 October 1965

Hacker, Jonathan, *Take Ten: Contemporary British Film Directors*, Oxford Paperbacks, 1991

Hayward, Anthony, *WHICH SIDE ARE YOU ON? Ken Loach and His Films*, Bloomsbury Publishing, 2005

Henri, Adrian, introduction to *Up the Junction*, Virago, 2013

http://www.screenonline.org.uk/tv/id/440997/index.html

https://www.youtube.com/watch?v=qzfoBN07JXI

https://en.wikipedia.org/wiki/Up_the_Junction_(The_Wednesday_Play)_

https://womensfilmandtelevisionhistory.wordpress.com/2016/06/10/poor-cow-1967/

https://thefword.org.uk/2016/06/it-was-such-a-laugh-writer-nell-dunn-in-conversation

http://tonygarnett.info/huw-wheldons-near-resignation-over-up-the-junction/

http://tonygarnett.info/sydney-newman-defends-the-wednesday-play/

https://www.bbc.co.uk/sounds/play/p01f6v7x (Margaret Drabble, Nell Dunn on *Woman's Hour*, August 2013)

https://www.bbc.co.uk/sounds/play/b037jfmj

https://www.bbc.co.uk/sounds/play/b07gh57x

https://www.youtube.com/watch?v=EC5jbuSylec

https://www.youtube.com/watch?v=qnxxDR5lIJc

https://www.newyorker.com/books/page-turner/the-secrets-of-the-forgotten-1965-classic-talking-to-women

https://bentleyrumble.blogspot.com/2015/07/nell-dunn-poor-cow-1967.html

https://www.imdb.com/title/tt0062141/

https://www.theguardian.com/lifeandstyle/2011/jul/09/nell-dunn-partner-home-death

Leigh, Jacob, *The Cinema of Ken Loach: Art in the Service of the People*, Wallflower Press, May 2002

Loach, Ken, *An Interview with Ken Loach*, Framework: The Journal of Cinema and Media, No. 18 (1982), pp. 9-12

Loach, Ken, *My first movie: twenty celebrated directors talk about their first film*, Pantheon Books, 2000

Playboy USA, June 1968

Poor Cow, film, 1967

Powell, Dilys, *Sunday Times*, 10 December 1967

Smith, Ali, Introduction to *Talking to Women*, Silver Press, May 2018

Street, Sarah, *The Colour of Social Realism*, Journal of British Cinema and Television, Vol 15, Issue 4, October 2018

Up the Junction, Wednesday Play, BBC, November 1965

Up the Junction, film, 1968

Waterman, Dennis, with Jill Arlon, *ReMinder*, Hutchinson, 2000

White, Carol, with Clifford Thurlow, *Carol Comes Home*, Hodder & Stoughton, 1 November 1982

White, Carol, New York Times interview, 10 February 1968

The Millstone: Margaret Drabble

A Touch of Love, film, 1969

Allardice, Lisa, *A life in writing: Margaret Drabble*, Guardian, 2011

Commire, Anne (editor), *Something About the Author*, Gale Research, 1987

Cooper-Clark Diana, *Interviews with Contemporary Novelists*, Palgrave Macmillan,1986

Cronan Rose, Ellen, *The Novels of Margaret Drabble: Equivocal Figures*, Macmillan, 1980

Cunningham, Gail, *Women and Children First: The novels of Margaret Drabble*, Twentieth-Century Women Novelists, The Macmillan Press, 1982

Drabble, Margaret, *Desert Island Discs*, BBC, 2001

Drabble, Margaret, *The Millstone*, Penguin, April 2010

Drabble, Margaret, *A Day in the Life of a Smiling Woman*, Penguin, June 2011

Drabble, Margaret, interview, BBC *World Book Club*, 2016

Drabble, Margaret, interview, *Meridian*, BBC Radio 4, 1996

Drabble, Margaret, interview with Jonathan Sale, Independent, 24 September 2009

Drabble, Margaret, interview with Dr Nick Turner, May 2010 (https://dspace.flinders.edu.au/xmlui/bitstream/handle/23 28/27260/Drabble_Turner.pdf?sequence=1)

Drabble, Margaret, *The Pattern in the Carpet*, Atlantic Books, 2009

Gerrard, Nicci, *Drabble and strife*, The Guardian, 2000

Grosvenor Myer, Valerie, *Margaret Drabble: A Reader's Guide*, Vision, 1991

Hardin, Nancy S, *An Interview With Margaret Drabble*, Contemporary Literature Vol. 14, No. 3, 1973

Hussein, Waris, *In conversation with... Ian McKellen and Waris Hussein on A Touch of Love*, BFI

https://www.scmp.com/magazines/post-magazine/books/article/1889202/novelist-margaret-drabble-talks-marrying-young-and

https://www.telegraph.co.uk/culture/books/8632911/Ma rgaret-Drabble-Its-sad-but-our-feud-is-beyond-repair.html

https://www.theguardian.com/books/2015/may/15/the-millstone-the-crucial-1960s-feminist-novel

https://www.theparisreview.org/interviews/3440/margar et-drabble-the-art-of-fiction-no-70-margaret-drabble

https://www.bbc.co.uk/sounds/play/p03m0x3t

https://www.independent.co.uk/arts-entertainment/books/features/margaret-drabble-the-original-angry-young-woman-2305790.html

https://www.theguardian.com/books/2011/mar/26/the-millstone-margaret-drabble-readers-responses

https://newrepublic.com/article/82624/millstone-margaret-drabble-adelle-waldman

https://www.bbc.co.uk/sounds/play/p00948vq

http://www.tcm.turner.com/tcmdb/title/92671/Thank-You-All-Very-Much/articles.html

https://www.youtube.com/watch?v=jM2eMeenIRs

Independent, *The original angry young woman*, 3 July 2011

Lambert, Angela, *Novelist Margaret Drabble on Illicit Love, Marriage and Motherhood*, Daily Mail, 1999

New York Times, *Thank You All Very Much*, film review, 1969

Phillips, Caroline, *Why Margaret Drabble says, 'I can live with my husband now'*, Evening Standard, February 1992

Spitzer, Susan, *Fantasy and Femaleness in Margaret Drabble's The Millstone*, A Forum on Fiction, Duke University Press, 1978

Georgy Girl: Margaret Forster

Adler, Tim, *The House of Redgrave: The Lives of a Theatrical Dynasty*, Aurum Press Ltd, 2014

Billington, Rachel, *The Great Umbilical*, Hutchinson, 1994

Davies, Hunter, *The Beatles, Football and Me*, Headline Review, 2006

Davies, Hunter, *A Life in the Day*, Simon and Schuster, 2017

Davies, Hunter, *Strong Lad Wanted for Strong Lass*, Bookcase, 2004

Forster, Margaret, *Georgy Girl*, Secker & Warburg, 1965

Forster, Margaret, *Desert Island Discs*, BBC Radio 4, 1994

Forster, Margaret, interview with Eleanor Wachtel, CBC, 1997

Forster, Margaret, *My Life in Houses*, Chatto & Windus, 2014

Forster, Margaret, *Techniques of Novel Writing*, The Writer, 1973

Forster, Margaret, *Hidden Lives: A Family Memoir*, Viking, 1995

Forster, Margaret, *Precious Lives*, Vintage, 1999

Forster, Margaret, *Good Wives? Mary, Fanny, Jennie and Me, 1845-2001*, Chatto & Windus, 2001

Georgy Girl, film, 1966

Grove, Valerie, *Margaret Forster: A northern lass in NW5*, New Statesman, March 2016

Grove, Valerie, *The Compleat Woman: Marriage, Motherhood, Career – Can She Have it All?* Chatto & Windus, 1987

https://www.imdb.com/title/tt0060453/

https://www.telegraph.co.uk/women/womens-life/9709488/Charlotte-Rampling-Im-not-interested-in-easy-parts.html

https://www.youtube.com/watch?v=KjoSLPRkspI (Judith Durham of the Seekers)

https://www.abc.net.au/news/2019-04-08/the-seeker-reunite-and-share-never-before-seen-archives/10879406 (Judith Durham of the Seekers)

https://www.youtube.com/watch?v=M3m_FhNfPKU&t=402s (Judith Durham, *This Is Your Life*, 1997)

https://www.theguardian.com/books/2017/jul/29/margaret-forster-hunter-davies-diaries

Jones, Kathleen, *Margaret Forster: A Life in Books*, The Book Mill, 2012

Mandelbaum, Ken, *Not Since Carrie: Forty Years of Broadway Musical Flops*, St Martin's Press, 2000

Mankiewicz, Tom, and Robert Crane, *My Life as a Mankiewicz: An Insider's Journey through Hollywood*, University Press of Kentucky, 2014

Nichols, Peter, *Diaries, 1969 – 1977*, Nick Hern Books, 2017

Redgrave, Lynn, *This is Living*, Dutton, 1991

Redgrave, Lynn, Foreword to *The Judith Durham Story: Colours of My Life*, Virgin Books, 2003

Simpson, Graham, *The Judith Durham Story: Colours of My Life*, Virgin Books, 2003

Spoto, Donald, *Otherwise Engaged: The Life of Alan Bates*, Arrow, 2008

General

Aldgate, Anthony, *Censorship and the Permissive Society: British Cinema and Theatre, 1955-1965*, Oxford University Press, 1991

Australian Women's Weekly

British Newspaper Archive

Canberra Times

Daily Mail

Daily Mirror

Groes, Sebastian, *British Fictions of the Sixties: The Making of the Swinging Decade*, Bloomsbury, 2009

Guardian

Illustrated London News

IMDb (https://www.imdb.com/)

Kensington Post

Life magazine

Maclean's magazine (Canada)

Monthly Film Bulletin, British Film Institute

Morrissey, *Autobiography*, Penguin Modern Classics, 2013

Observer

Philips, Deborah, *Women's Fiction from 1945 to Today*, Bloomsbury Academic, 2014

Sight and Sound

Sunday Times

Tatler

Times Literary Supplement

Trevelyan, John, *What the censor saw*, Michael Joseph Ltd, 1973

Walker, Alexander, *Hollywood England, The British Film Industry in the Sixties*, Orion Books Ltd, 2005

Mary Eagleton, *The History of British Women's Writing, 1945-1975*, Volume Nine, Palgrave Macmillan, 2017

Printed in Great Britain
by Amazon

29315211R00158